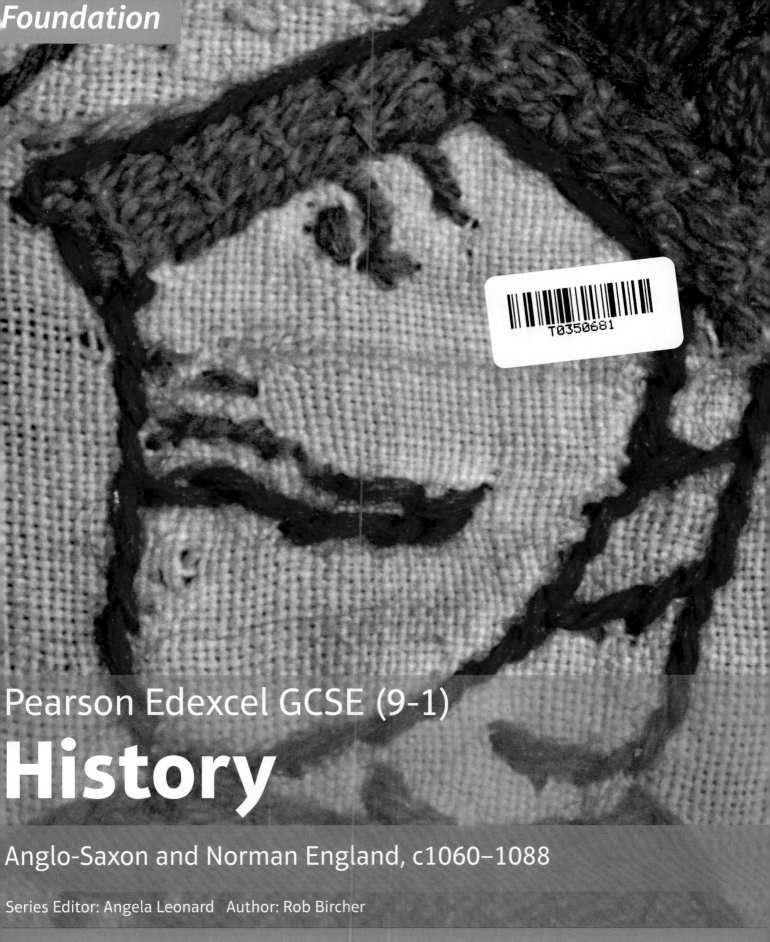

Foundation

Pearson Edexcel GCSE (9-1)

History

Anglo-Saxon and Norman England, c1060–1088

Series Editor: Angela Leonard   Author: Rob Bircher

P Pearson

Published by Pearson Education Limited,
80 Strand, London, WC2R 0RL.

www.pearsonschoolsandfecolleges.co.uk

Copies of official specifications for all Pearson qualifications
may be found on the website: qualifications.pearson.com

Text © Pearson Education Limited 2020

Series editor: Angela Leonard
Produced by Florence Production Ltd, Devon, UK
Typeset by Florence Production Ltd, Devon, UK
Original illustrations © Pearson Education Limited
Illustrated by KJA Artists Illustration Agency,
Phoenix Photosetting, Chatham, Kent, and
Florence Production Ltd, Devon

Picture research by Integra
Cover photo © Alamy Images: Robert Harding Picture
Library Ltd

The right of Rob Bircher to be identified as author of this
work has been asserted by him in accordance with the
Copyright, Designs and Patents Act 1988.

First published 2020

23 22 21 20
10 9 8 7 6 5 4 3 2 1

British Library Cataloguing in Publication Data
A catalogue record for this book is available from the
British Library.

ISBN 978 1 292 35012 7

Printed in Slovakia by Neografia

A note from the publisher
1. While the publishers have made every attempt to ensure
that advice on the qualifications and assessment is accurate,
the official specification and associated guidance materials are
the only authoritative source of information and should always
be referred to for definitive guidance. Pearson examiners have
not contributed to any sections in this resource relevant to
examination papers for which they have responsibility.

2. Pearson has robust editorial processes, including answer
and fact checks, to ensure the accuracy of the content in
this publication, and every effort is made to ensure this
publication is free of errors. We are, however, only human,
and occasionally errors do occur. Pearson is not liable for
any misunderstandings that arise as a result of errors in this
publication, but it is our priority to ensure that the content
is accurate. If you spot an error, please do contact us at
resourcescorrections@pearson.com so we can make sure it is
corrected.

Websites
Pearson Education Limited is not responsible for the content
of any external internet sites. It is essential for tutors to
preview each website before using it in class so as to ensure
that the URL is still accurate, relevant and appropriate. We
suggest that tutors bookmark useful websites and consider
enabling students to access them through the school/college
intranet.

Contents

How to use this book

What's covered?

This book covers the British Depth study on Anglo-Saxon and Norman England, c1060–88. This unit makes up 20% of your GCSE course, and will be examined in Paper 2.

Depth studies cover a short period of time, and require you to know about society, people and events in detail. You need to understand how the different aspects of the period fit together and affect each other. This book also explains the different types of exam questions you will need to answer, and includes advice and example answers to help you improve.

Features

As well as a clear, detailed explanation of the key knowledge you will need, you will also find a number of features in the book:

Key terms

Where you see a word followed by an asterisk, like this: Housecarls*, you will be able to find a Key Terms box on that page that explains what the word means.

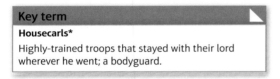

Key term

Housecarls*

Highly-trained troops that stayed with their lord wherever he went; a bodyguard.

Activities

Every few pages, you'll find a box containing some activities designed to help check and embed knowledge and get you to really think about what you've studied. The activities start simple, but might get more challenging as you work through them.

Summaries and Checkpoints

At the end of each chunk of learning, the main points are summarised in a series of bullet points – great for embedding the core knowledge, and handy for revision.

Checkpoints help you to check and reflect on your learning. The Strengthen section helps you to consolidate knowledge and understanding, and check that you've grasped the basic ideas and skills. The Challenge questions push you to go beyond just understanding the information, and into evaluation and analysis of what you've studied.

Sources and Interpretations

Although source work and interpretations do not appear in Paper 2, you'll still find interesting contemporary material throughout the book, showing what people from the period said, thought or created, helping you to build your understanding of people in the past.

The book also includes extracts from the work of historians, showing how experts have interpreted the events you've been studying.

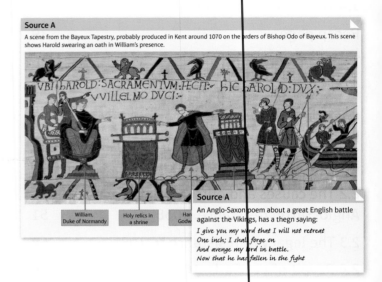

Source A

A scene from the Bayeux Tapestry, probably produced in Kent around 1070 on the orders of Bishop Odo of Bayeux. This scene shows Harold swearing an oath in William's presence.

William, Duke of Normandy | Holy relics in a shrine | Harold Godwinson

Source A

An Anglo-Saxon poem about a great English battle against the Vikings, has a thegn saying:

I give you my word that I will not retreat
One inch; I shall forge on
And avenge my lord in battle.
Now that he has fallen in the fight

Exam-style questions and tips

The book also includes extra exam-style questions you can use to practise. These appear in the chapters and are accompanied by a tip to help you get started on an answer.

Exam-style question, Section B

Describe **two** features of the social system of Anglo-Saxon England.   **4 marks**

Exam tip

You need to identify two relevant points and then develop each point. For example: 'The social system was not fixed. This meant a free peasant who did very well could become a thegn.'

Other features you could develop:

- There were slaves in Anglo-Saxon society. People became slaves when…
- The most important aristocrats were called earls. Earls ruled…
- Thegns were local lords. A thegn needed to own…

Recap pages

At the end of each chapter, you'll find a page designed to help you to consolidate and reflect on the chapter as a whole. Each recap page includes a recall quiz, ideal for quickly checking your knowledge or for revision. Recap pages also include activities designed to help you summarise and analyse what you've learned, and also reflect on how each chapter links to other parts of the unit.

THINKING HISTORICALLY

These activities are designed to help you develop a better understanding of how history is constructed, and are focused on the key areas of Evidence, Interpretations, Cause & Consequence and Change & Continuity. In the British Depth Study, you will come across activities on Cause & Consequence, as this is a key focus for this unit.

The Thinking Historically approach has been developed in conjunction with Dr Arthur Chapman and the Institute of Education, UCL. It is based on research into the misconceptions that can hold students back in history.

THINKING HISTORICALLY **Cause and Consequence (3a&b)** — conceptual map reference

The Thinking Historically conceptual map can be found at: www.pearsonschools.co.uk/thinkinghistoricallygcse

WRITING HISTORICALLY

At the end of most chapters is a spread dedicated to helping you improve your writing skills. These include simple techniques you can use in your writing to make your answers clearer, more precise and better focused on the question you're answering.

The Writing Historically approach is based on the *Grammar for Writing* teaching method developed by a team at the University of Exeter and popular in many English departments. Each spread uses examples from the preceding chapter, so it's relevant to what you've just been studying.

Preparing for your exams

At the back of the book, you'll find a special section dedicated to explaining and exemplifying the new Edexcel GCSE History exams. Advice on the demands of this paper, written by Angela Leonard, helps you prepare for and approach the exam with confidence. Each question type is explained through annotated sample answers at two levels, showing clearly how answers can be improved.

Pearson Progression Scale: This icon indicates the Step that a sample answer has been graded at on the Pearson Progression Scale.

Timeline: Anglo-Saxons and Normans

Anglo-Saxon

Norman

Edward the Confessor: 1042–1066

Harold II: 1066

William I: 1066–1087

Non-military events

1050
Earl Godwin exiled after refusing to obey Edward the Confessor
Edward possibly makes a deal with William of Normandy about succession

1051
Edward makes Godwin Earl of Wessex again

1053
Death of Earl Godwin; Harold Godwinson becomes Earl of Wessex

1055
Tostig Godwinson made Earl of Northumbria

1064
Harold's embassy to Normandy

1065
Tostig exiled

1067
William returns to Normandy to celebrate his victory; he returns to England in December

1067
Bishop Odo made Earl of Kent; co-regent of England

1066
Death of Edward the Confessor; Harold becomes king

1066
25 December – William crowned king of England; lands forfeited to the new king

1050	1055	1060	1065

1051
Earl Godwin returns to England with an army

1062
The Godwins defeat the Welsh king, Gruffudd ap Llywelyn

1065
Uprising against Earl Tostig

1068
Revolt of Earls Edwin and Morcar

1066
20 September – The Battle of Gate Fulford
25 September – The Battle of Stamford Bridge
28 September – Normans land at Pevensey Bay
14 October – Battle of Hastings

1069
Rebellions in the North

1069–70
Harrying of the North

Military events

William II (William Rufus):
1087–1100

1070
Stigand replaced by Lanfranc as Archbishop of Canterbury

1071
Edwin's lands forfeited

1076
Inquiry into Bishop Odo's illegal land grabs

1080
Robert and William reconciled

1082
Bishop Odo imprisoned

1083
Death of Matilda, William's wife and trusted regent

1084
Heavy geld tax levied

1085
William orders Domesday Book surveys

1086
First drafts of the Domesday Book shown to William; landholders summoned to swear allegiance

1087
Death of William in Normandy William II (William Rufus) crowned king of England

070   1075   1080   1085   1090

1070–71
Hereward the Wake and the revolt at Ely

1075
Revolt of the Earls

1077
Robert Curthose rebels against his father, William

1085
Threat of Danish invasion means William brings thousands more troops into England

1088
Odo leads rebellion against William Rufus, which is defeated

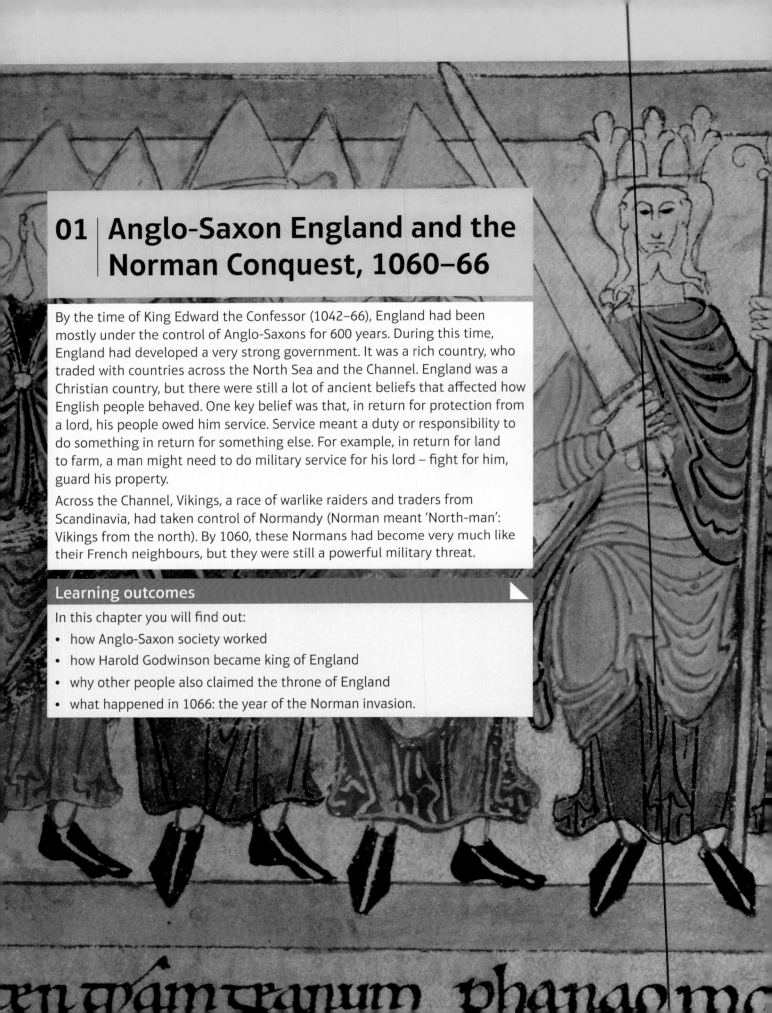

01 | Anglo-Saxon England and the Norman Conquest, 1060–66

By the time of King Edward the Confessor (1042–66), England had been mostly under the control of Anglo-Saxons for 600 years. During this time, England had developed a very strong government. It was a rich country, who traded with countries across the North Sea and the Channel. England was a Christian country, but there were still a lot of ancient beliefs that affected how English people behaved. One key belief was that, in return for protection from a lord, his people owed him service. Service meant a duty or responsibility to do something in return for something else. For example, in return for land to farm, a man might need to do military service for his lord – fight for him, guard his property.

Across the Channel, Vikings, a race of warlike raiders and traders from Scandinavia, had taken control of Normandy (Norman meant 'North-man': Vikings from the north). By 1060, these Normans had become very much like their French neighbours, but they were still a powerful military threat.

Learning outcomes

In this chapter you will find out:

- how Anglo-Saxon society worked
- how Harold Godwinson became king of England
- why other people also claimed the throne of England
- what happened in 1066: the year of the Norman invasion.

1.1 Anglo-Saxon society

Learning outcomes

- Understand the Anglo-Saxon social system and the power of the monarch.
- Understand how England was governed and the role of the Church.
- Understand the economy of Anglo-Saxon England.

What was England like in 1060?

- Very few people – only about 2 million in the whole of England.
- Almost everyone farmed and lived off what they grew.
- The aristocracy* were at the top of Anglo-Saxon* society.
- Slaves were at the bottom of Anglo-Saxon society.

Key terms

Aristocracy*
The people in society who were important because they had inherited their wealth and power.

Anglo-Saxon*
People who had settled in England after the Romans left Britain.

Service*
Doing something in return for receiving something else you want, for example farming someone else's land in return for land to farm for yourself.

The social system

Peasant farmers

Most Anglo-Saxons were peasant farmers. They rented small farms that they worked for themselves and their families.

Peasants did a set amount of work for the local lord as well as working their own land. This was called service*. If they did not carry out this work for their lord then the peasants could lose their right to use their rented land.

No one used land without carrying out some kind of service to someone else.

Slaves

10% of the Anglo-Saxon population were slaves. Slaves could be bought and sold. They were seen more like property than people. The Normans thought that owning slaves was barbaric, but it was a normal part of Anglo-Saxon society.

Thegns

Thegns were the local lords. There were between 4,000 and 5,000 thegns by 1060.

A thegn was an important man in the local community. Thegns were the aristocracy of the Anglo-Saxon age, its warrior class.

To be a thegn, a man needed a manor house with a tower and a church. He also needed more than five hides* of land.

Key term

Hides*
The measurement used for land in Anglo-Saxon and Norman England. One hide was about 120 acres: the amount a family needed to support themselves.

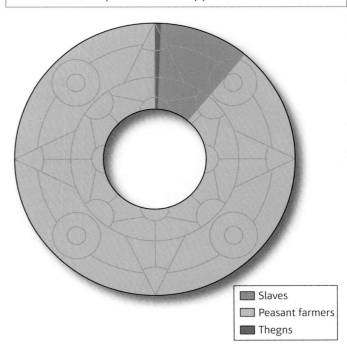

Slaves
Peasant farmers
Thegns

Figure 1.1 The social structure of Anglo-Saxon England. Around 10% of the population were slaves, and almost everyone else was a peasant!

Summary

- 90% of Anglo-Saxons were peasants.
- Peasants rented land from their lord in return for work.
- Local lords were called thegns. Thegns were warriors.
- At the top of the social system were the aristocrats.
- Slaves were at the bottom of the social system.

Earls

Earls* were the most important aristocrats: the most important men in the country after the king. The earls competed against each other to be the one the king trusted and relied on the most. The king would reward his most reliable and trusted earls with land and money. Sometimes, earls even challenged the king to get more power.

Figure 1.2 The main earldoms of England in 1060.

Key term

Earls*

Highest Anglo-Saxon aristocracy. An earl ruled a large area for the king. The area controlled by an earl is called an earldom.

Changing social status

It was possible to change your status in Anglo-Saxon society.

- Slaves could be freed by their masters and become peasants.
- People could also move down – for example, peasants could sell themselves into slavery, especially if their family would starve to death if they didn't.
- A peasant who did very well and got five hides of land could become a thegn.
- Merchants who made a number of trips abroad in their own ships could also become thegns.
- At the top of the social system, thegns could be raised to the status of earls. Earls could sometimes even become kings.

Exam-style question, Section B

Describe **two** features of the social system of Anglo-Saxon England.   **4 marks**

Exam tip

You need to identify two relevant points and then develop each point. For example: 'The social system was not fixed. This meant a free peasant who did very well could become a thegn.'

Other features you could develop:

- There were slaves in Anglo-Saxon society. People became slaves when…
- The most important aristocrats were called earls. Earls ruled…
- Thegns were local lords. A thegn needed to own…

The power of the English monarchy

In 1060, the king (monarch) was Edward the Confessor. He was the most powerful person in Anglo-Saxon England. He governed the country.

Powers of the king

Law-making: the king created new laws.

Money: the king controlled the production of the silver pennies used as money.

Landownership: the king owned all the land. He could give land out to loyal followers. He could take land away as a punishment.

Military power: the king could raise a national army and a fleet of ships.

Taxation: the king said when taxes had to be paid. The tax went to the king.

Duties of the people

To obey the law.

Only to use the king's coins. Forging coins was a very serious crime.

People who got land from the king had to fight for him in return.

Landholders had to provide fighters and their weapons for the army.

Landholders had to pay their taxes, otherwise they were fined or lost their land.

Figure 1.3 The powers of Edward the Confessor and the duties of his people. The image in the middle is Edward's royal seal. This seal was attached to his royal orders to show they came from the king.

The king's role was to protect his people from attack and give them laws to keep them safe. In return, the people of England had to obey his laws.

Every boy swore an oath* when they reached 12 years of age to be faithful to the king. The oath was made to the shire reeve* at a special ceremony held each year (see Source A).

Edward the Confessor as a leader

Edward the Confessor was a religious leader, not a warrior king, but his earls and their thegns were a powerful military force. He relied on his earls, especially Earl Godwin, to protect England from attack.

Although King Edward was not a warrior, he was respected for two other things:

- **he was a good law-maker** – Anglo-Saxons respected rulers who kept things peaceful
- **he was very religious** – Anglo-Saxons thought that a religious king would mean that God would look after the kingdom.

Source A

The oath sworn by Anglo-Saxon boys once they reached 12 years of age.

All shall swear in the name of the Lord, before whom every holy thing is holy, that they will be faithful to the king.

Key terms

Oath*

A solemn promise to do something. Anglo-Saxons swore oaths on holy relics to make them especially important not to break. A relic was often a body part of a dead saint, kept in a special chest.

Shire reeve*

An official of the king: his sheriff. Shire reeves managed the king's lands, collected taxes for him and were in charge of local courts.

Limits to the king's power

The Danelaw

Half of England was called the Danelaw* (see the map on page 10). Most people who lived here had Viking ancestors.

Although those who lived in the Danelaw part of England accepted the rule of the king, they had some different laws and customs. They also preferred it if their earls and government officials were also from the Danelaw.

The power of Earl Godwin

This story of King Edward and Earl Godwin, Earl of Wessex, shows that King Edward's powers could be quite limited.

Wessex was the richest earldom of England and Godwin and his family owned so much land that they were as rich as the king. They had many thegns so had powerful armies. Earl Godwin forced King Edward into decisions that were good for the Godwins. For example, to appoint Godwin's followers to important Church positions or give earldoms to his sons.

Earl Godwin's challenge in 1050

Godwin and Edward's power struggle

- People from Dover (in Godwin's earldom of Wessex) attacked a visiting embassy* from Boulogne.
- King Edward ordered Earl Godwin to punish the people of Dover.
- Godwin refused.
- King Edward got two other earls (Siward of Northumbria and Leofric of Mercia) to help him force Godwin to go into exile*.
- In 1051, Godwin returned with a fleet of ships and an army.
- Godwin demanded his earldom back from King Edward.
- To prevent war with Godwin, King Edward agreed.

Activities

1 While you are at school, your teacher (your lord) provides you with education and looks after your well-being. What duties do you owe your teacher in return?

2 Describe one way the king could protect England from foreign invasions.

3 Explain one way earls could challenge the king's power. (The story of Earl Godwin will help with this question.)

Key terms

The Danelaw*

The part of England where Danish (Viking) power had been strongest and which had kept some of its Danish laws instead of Anglo-Saxon ones. You can see the area occupied by the Danelaw in Figure 1.2 on page 10.

Embassy*

An official visit by representatives of one ruler to another ruler.

Exile*

To exile someone meant to force them to leave the country.

Archbishop*

The chief bishop of a large region.

Government

The Witan

The Witan was a council that gave the king advice. It was made up of the most important aristocrats of the kingdom, including earls and archbishops*. It discussed:

- possible threats from foreign powers
- religious affairs
- land disputes and how to settle them.

The Witan also had an important role in approving a new king, which we will look at later (page 28).

The king did not have to follow the Witan's advice. The king also decided who was in the Witan and when it met.

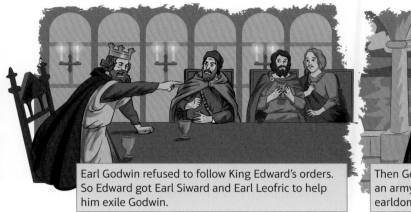

Earl Godwin refused to follow King Edward's orders. So Edward got Earl Siward and Earl Leofric to help him exile Godwin.

Then Godwin came back to England with a fleet and an army. King Edward was forced to give Godwin his earldom back – or face a war.

▶ Earl Godwin and King Edward's relationship.

Source B

The king and his Witan. This image is from an 11th-century book of Old Testament Bible stories.

ꝼꞇꝛ ꞇꞃꝭm ꞡꞃꝭum phaꞃꝭao mœꞇꞇe ꝫꝛꝥꝫ ꞇꝺꝛ beꞃꝭne ꞇꝛ ꝭhꞇm ꝉꝺ ....

Summary

Features of the Witan

- It was a council.
- It gave advice to the king, e.g. about threats from other countries.
- Made up of the kingdom's most important men.
- The king did not have to follow its advice.
- The Witan had a role in agreeing who became king.

Earldoms

What power did earls have?

The earls were given many of the powers of the king to help him rule the country.

These powers gave the earls economic, legal and military control of their earldoms. The big earldoms (see Figure 1.2) had a huge amount of power.

Key term

Housecarls*

Highly-trained troops that stayed with their lord wherever he went; a bodyguard.

Earls collected taxes for the king from their earldom. They kept one-third of these taxes.

Earls judged crimes in their earldom. They decided punishments.

They were supposed to use the money from taxes to improve their earldoms, e.g. build defences.

Earls were the king's military leaders.

They had hundreds of thegns plus a bodyguard of housecarls*.

The money they kept from taxes also made them very rich men.

▶ The king gave earls some of his powers so they could rule their earldoms for him.

Limits to the earls' powers

When a king was strong, the power of the earls was definitely less than that of the king. A powerful king would demand obedience and would punish those who failed him. But Edward the Confessor was not strong.

The earls also had to be careful not to upset their thegns too often. We know this because there were times when thegns demanded that earls be removed from their positions. This happened in 1065 when Earl Tostig, the son of Godwin, lost his earldom and went into exile when his thegns complained about the way he governed his earldom, Northumbria. There is more about this story on page 23.

Exam-style question, Section B ○

Describe **two** features of earldoms in Anglo-Saxon England.   **4 marks**

Exam tip ○

A feature is something that is special or characteristic – we tell the difference between one person and another, for example, by recognising their different facial features. So, when a question asks for two features of earldoms, think about the things that made earldoms different – their special characteristics. Remember to develop each point to explain the feature.

Summary ◤

- Earls took over some of the king's powers to rule their earldoms for the king.
- They collected tax (and kept a third).
- They provided law and order (but did not make new laws).
- They were the king's generals and had many warrior followers – thegns.
- If a king was weak, like King Edward, then earls could become very powerful (Earl Godwin is a good example of this).
- If an earl badly upset his thegns, he could lose his earldom. (Earl Tostig Godwinson is an example of this.)

Local government

The shire

Earldoms were divided into shires. Shires had social, political, economic and military roles.

- **Social:** each shire had its own court for trying cases and giving punishments.
- **Political:** the shire reeve acted as the king's representative in the shire (see next page).
- **Economic:** each shire had a burh (fortified town). On the next page you can see how they were important.
- **Military:** each shire provided troops for the fyrd* (see below).

The hundred and the hide

Shires were divided into **hundreds***, and hundreds into **tithings*** – units of ten households. At the base of the whole administrative system was the hide. Each hide of land meant the person renting or owning it had to pay: taxes and provide military service.

Key terms ◤

Fyrd*

The men of the Anglo-Saxon army and fleet. Every five hides provided one man for the fyrd.

Hundreds*

A unit of land administration. In some parts of England, a hundred was 100 hides of land, but in other areas it didn't have this direct connection.

Tithings*

An administrative unit that was a group of ten households – originally equivalent to a tenth of a hundred in some areas.

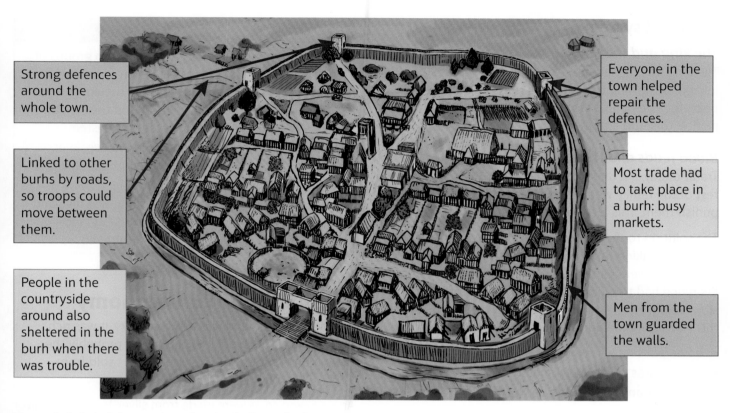

Strong defences around the whole town.

Linked to other burhs by roads, so troops could move between them.

People in the countryside around also sheltered in the burh when there was trouble.

Everyone in the town helped repair the defences.

Most trade had to take place in a burh: busy markets.

Men from the town guarded the walls.

Figure 1.4 Artist's impression of an Anglo-Saxon burh.

Shire reeves

The shire reeves, or sheriffs, were the king's local government officials and they worked within the earldoms to look after the king's interests. Their duties included:

- collecting revenues* from the king's land
- collecting the geld tax*
- collecting fines from the shire court
- making sure people obeyed the law at the shire court
- providing men for the fyrd
- repairing roads and fortifications.

The king gave orders to the shire reeves through writs*.

Military service – the fyrd

When the call came from the king, each group of five hides had to provide one man for the fyrd, together with his battle equipment. There were two types of fyrd:

- the **select** fyrd gathered men to fight anywhere in England for the king
- the **general** fyrd gathered men to fight who didn't travel outside their local area.

The select fyrd was just made up of thegns and their followers. The thegns probably trained together and were well-equipped with weapons, armour and horses. However, these men could only stay away from home for a few weeks before their farms would suffer – especially at harvest time, which needed everyone in the area to work together. A period of 40 days was fixed for their service, after which a fyrd would be disbanded – that meant everyone would be sent back home.

Key terms

Revenues*

Money that is paid in: also called income. Revenues were taxes coming into the king's treasury.

Geld tax*

A tax on land, originally to pay off the Vikings (Danegeld). It went to the king.

Writs*

Written instructions with a seal stamped by the king.

The legal system

The king and the law

The king was the law-maker. The people of England looked to the king to make laws that kept things peaceful. The people also expected the king to provide justice: to settle arguments in a fair way.

Blood feuds and Wergild

Traditionally, if a family member was attacked, then the rest of the family would find the person responsible and punish them. This led to blood feuds*.

The solution to the blood feud problem was Wergild. Instead of taking revenge, the family who had suffered the murder were paid money by the murderer's family. Everyone had to follow Wergild, so it was a fair system. However, the more important the murdered person was, the more Wergild had to be paid. For example:

- a free peasant was worth 20 shillings
- a thegn was worth 1,200 shillings
- an earl or an archbishop was worth 3,600 shillings.

It is difficult to make direct comparisons with our money today, but some historians suggest 1 shilling would be worth about £100 today.

Collective responsibility

When a crime was committed, all the members of a tithing had to hunt for the criminal. This was called the 'hue and cry'. The men of the tithing were also responsible for the good behaviour of their ten households. If someone was proved to have done something wrong, they all had to pay a fine. If, for example, someone from their village refused to join the general fyrd, there would be consequences for everyone in the tithing. This is called 'collective responsibility'.

Activities ?

1 Imagine that your class is divided into groups of ten and that you are collectively responsible for each other's behaviour. What are the advantages of this system for your teacher and the school? Are there any disadvantages to the system?

2 Come up with one strength and one weakness of the fyrd system for defending Anglo-Saxon England from attack.

3 Describe how each of the following was involved in the government of Anglo-Saxon England.
   a Earls   b Shire reeves

The Anglo-Saxon economy

Anglo-Saxon England was a rich country. It was rich because of trade. Wool and cloth were probably the most important English exports (goods sold from England to other countries).

Anglo-Saxon coins were made from silver. Most of the silver used for coins was dug up in Germany. Perhaps Anglo-Saxon traders exchanged this silver for wool and cloth.

Another interesting example of trade is wine. Anglo-Saxons drank wine made in Normandy. So there must have been trade between England and Normandy.

Anglo-Saxons were also good at farming crops. There was a well-organised system for making flour – there were more than 6,000 mills.

Key term

Blood feuds*

If someone was killed, the victim's family had the right to kill someone from the murderer's family, who then had the right to revenge themselves, and so on.

▶ A picture from the Anglo-Saxon Calendar for the month of May. It shows shepherds watching their sheep. Sheep were very important for the English economy. England became famous for its woollen cloth during the medieval period.

Source C

An Anglo-Saxon silver penny from Edward the Confessor's reign. The coin shows Edward sitting on his throne. He is holding an orb (the ball-shaped object) and a sceptre. These symbols of royalty are still used by the British monarchy today.

Towns

- In 1066, around 10% of the population of England lived in towns.
- Each shire had its main town called a burh, which was well defended.
- These fortified burhs were planned so that no one was more than 15 or 20 miles from safety if they heard a viking raiding party was coming.
- The burhs were linked by roads so that troops could move quickly from one burh to another. They had strong walls and ramparts (steep earth banks) guarded by men from the town (see Figure 1.4).
- Administration and upkeep of the town and its fortifications was the responsibility of the burh's inhabitants.
- London and York were the biggest towns in England, with populations of more than 10,000 people.
- Towns like Norwich and Lincoln had populations of around 6,000 people.

Towns and trade

The burhs were also trading hubs. The king's laws demanded that all trade worth more than a set amount of money should take place in a burh, so that trade tax could be paid.

Towns often grew in importance because of international trading links. London was probably the biggest trading hub of all, with traders from Germany, France, Normandy and Flanders.

Villages

Most villages, houses and farms were not grouped together but spread out over the countryside. The houses were made of wood and thatched with straw, and were homes for lots of relatives living together rather than just one family. Most thegns lived in the countryside too. Their manor houses were larger and better built than peasant huts. Some of these manor houses may have been fortified against attack.

Thegns built a church and employed a priest to hold services for the thegn's household. These churches would also provide services for the surrounding area.

Summary

- Anglo-Saxon England was rich because of trade.
- Wool and cloth were probably its most important exports.
- Towns (burhs) were centres for trading.
- Tax was collected from traders – this shows how organised the Anglo-Saxon economy was.
- Anglo-Saxon England traded with many other countries including Normandy and what is now Germany.

The influence of the Church

An old-fashioned Church

Anglo-Saxon England was a Christian country. However, to a Norman it would have seemed very old-fashioned.

- In Normandy, Church reforms (modernisations) were common. England did not want to change its traditions.
- England had lots of old Anglo-Saxon saints the Normans didn't think were proper Christian saints.
- However, these old saints were very important to people. Often, people had their own local saints no one else really knew about.

How was the Church organised?

- The Church divided England into large areas with each area controlled by a bishop.
- Bishops were often rich, important people.
- Bishops and archbishops could be in the Witan.
- Bishops did not like it when thegns hired priests for their own churches – bishops wanted to control this.
- Local priests were usually ordinary members of the community.
- Local priests were usually married (Normans thought priests should not get married) and worked their own land, like peasants.
- Often local priests were not very well educated – many could not read Latin, even though this was the language of the Church.

England also had monasteries and nunneries: these were religious communities of monks and nuns run by abbots and abbesses. Unlike in Normandy, monasteries were in decline with monks becoming part of their local communities rather than living separate, holy lives apart from the world.

How important was religion?

Religion in Anglo-Saxon England was an important part of everyday life. The influence of the Church was very strong because people were worried about what would happen when they died. Everyone believed that they would spend time in the afterlife being punished for their sins. They believed you could reduce how long this punishment went on for by praying in Church.

English people believed God would be quick to punish countries for the sinful behaviour of their people, especially sinfulness within the Church or monarchy.

1.1 Anglo-Saxon society: summary

- The Anglo-Saxon Church was old-fashioned, compared with the Norman Church.
- Bishops were in charge of large areas. Bishops were very important and could be in the Witan.
- Local priests often lived like peasants: they farmed, were usually married and were not educated.
- Anglo-Saxon people believed that God would punish a whole country if its leaders were sinful.

Checkpoint

Strengthen

S1 Describe the differences between slaves, peasants, thegns and earls.

S2 Write a paragraph on 'a day in the life of a shire reeve'. Think about the duties that they were expected to perform.

S3 Explain what one of the following was: geld tax, the fyrd, a burh.

Challenge

C1 Summarise three ways in which the Anglo-Saxon king was more powerful than his earls.

Activity

Focused listing is a useful study skill to develop. Here's how it works:

a Write out the main Topic headings, e.g. Anglo-Saxon society, The power of the monarchy, Government, etc.

b For each one, read quickly through the text and then close the book.

c Then, for each heading, make a list of the main points you can recall about it.

d Check back through the book to see what you left out.

Use this method to make notes on the 'Government' and 'Economy' of Anglo-Saxon England sections.

Timeline

The last years of Edward the Confessor

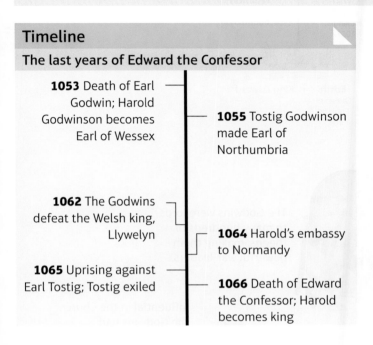

1053 Death of Earl Godwin; Harold Godwinson becomes Earl of Wessex

1055 Tostig Godwinson made Earl of Northumbria

1062 The Godwins defeat the Welsh king, Llywelyn

1064 Harold's embassy to Normandy

1065 Uprising against Earl Tostig; Tostig exiled

1066 Death of Edward the Confessor; Harold becomes king

The house of Godwin

The house of Godwin* began in 1018 during King Cnut's reign, when Cnut made his favourite adviser, Godwin, Earl of Wessex. Godwin was probably the son of an Anglo-Saxon thegn.

Political power in Anglo-Saxon England was increased by family connections. Godwin had helped Edward the Confessor to become king and, in return, the king married Godwin's daughter, Edith of Wessex, in 1045.

Key term

House of Godwin*
The 'house' of Godwin refers to the Godwin family.

Godwin control of England

- In 1053, Harold Godwinson succeeded his father as Earl of Wessex, giving Harold riches, influence over hundreds of thegns and a powerful position as adviser to the king.

- In 1055, Tostig Godwinson (Harold's brother) became the new Earl of Northumbria. That gave the Godwins a powerbase in the far north of England.

- In 1057, the earldom of East Anglia was given to Gyrth Godwinson, Harold's teenage brother.

- Also in 1057, a smaller earldom in the south-west Midlands went to Leofwine Godwinson – another younger brother of Harold.

Why did Edward allow it?

- Edward's marriage to Edith meant he was now related to the Godwins. Families help each other.

- England was under threat from Norway, meaning that Edward needed his earls to be strong military leaders. That is probably the reason why Tostig was made Earl of Northumbria instead of the old earl's son, Waltheof, who was too young to lead men into battle.

- Harold's marriage to Edith the Fair (another Edith), daughter of Aelfgar Earl of Mercia, may also have influenced the Godwins' getting the earldom of East Anglia, as Edith the Fair had inherited a lot of land in East Anglia.

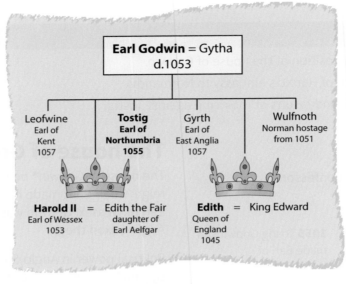

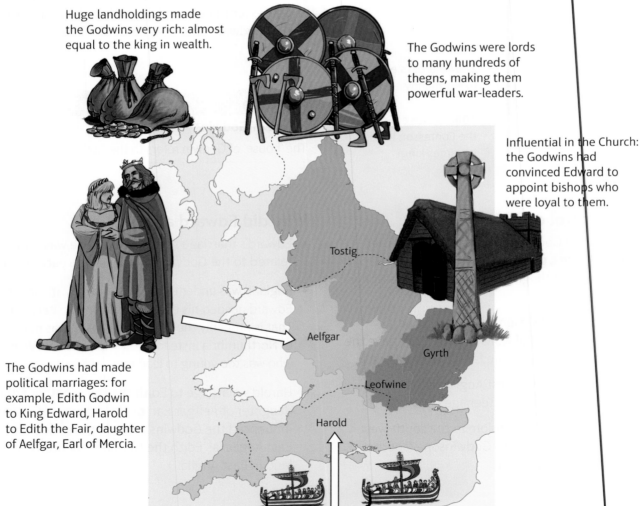

The power of the Godwins in 1060.

Huge landholdings made the Godwins very rich: almost equal to the king in wealth.

The Godwins were lords to many hundreds of thegns, making them powerful war-leaders.

Influential in the Church: the Godwins had convinced Edward to appoint bishops who were loyal to them.

The Godwins had made political marriages: for example, Edith Godwin to King Edward, Harold to Edith the Fair, daughter of Aelfgar, Earl of Mercia.

Wessex was England's defence zone against attacks across the Channel. Harold was also Earl of Hereford, which was often attacked from Wales. Holding these two earldoms made Harold important.

Figure 1.5 The power of the Godwins in 1060.

Activities

1 Look at the statements in the boxes to the right. They are all about the different ways in which the Godwins were powerful. Sort them into these three categories:
   - economic power (wealth)
   - military power
   - political power.

2 Pick one political, one military and one economic statement from your list. Explain why you put each in this category. For example:

   Harold was married to Edith the Fair, daughter of the Earl of Mercia. This was political power because it meant Harold was related to a powerful Earl.

> The Godwins owned land all across England.

> Many English bishops were loyal to the Godwins.

> Tostig was married to Judith of Flanders.

> Edith Godwin was married to King Edward.

> Harold commanded defences in Wessex and Hereford.

> The Godwins were almost as rich as King Edward.

> Harold was married to Edith the Fair, daughter of Aelfgar, Earl of Mercia.

> The Godwins had hundreds of thegns.

Military success

In 1062, Harold led a surprise attack against the king of Wales, Llywelyn. King Llywelyn escaped. Harold took a fleet round the coast of South Wales while his brother Tostig led an army overland into North Wales.

Their joint strategy was a brilliant success. Llywelyn was killed. Harold sent Llywelyn's head to Edward the Confessor. Harold himself then appointed a new king for Wales whom he could control. Harold was now King Edward's deputy: the leader of his armies and the most powerful of Edward's earls.

Godwin and the king

- Edward showed signs earlier in his reign of trying to get free from Godwin's control.
- In 1042, he had appointed some Normans to important positions, causing conflict with earls like Godwin.
- Norman sources say Edward promised the English throne to William of Normandy after his death, in return for William's support against Godwin.
- However, it is not clear how Normans helped Edward with taking on Godwin, because Godwin was returned to power in 1051 and his sons were given the most powerful positions in the kingdom.

Harold's embassy to Normandy

Harold Godwinson went to Normandy in the early summer of 1064 (or possibly 1065) on a mission for King Edward – a type of visit called an embassy.

- Harold travelled to France, but landed in Ponthieu, a small county between Normandy and Flanders – perhaps blown off-course by a storm.
- Harold was taken prisoner by Count Guy of Ponthieu.
- Duke William heard of the capture and demanded that Guy hand Harold over.
- Harold then spent time with William in Normandy, and helped him in two military campaigns.
- William gave Harold gifts of weapons and armour to say thanks for his help. These gifts were symbolic of the relationship between a lord and his warrior.

Harold then made a solemn oath to William, swearing on two holy relics. This *could* have been Harold swearing to support William's claim to the throne of England.

Anglo-Saxons and Normans both had different ideas about why Harold was sent on this embassy.

- The Normans said that Harold went to talk to Duke William about plans for William's succession. As part of this, Harold swore to follow William as his king, after Edward died.
- The Anglo-Saxon view was Harold went to recover two hostages* from William – Harold's brother and his nephew: Wulfnoth and Hakon.

Harold's embassy to Normandy is difficult to interpret, but it is important in three main ways:

- It shows that Harold was King Edward's trusted adviser, as this was clearly an important embassy, whatever its aim was.
- It was used by the Normans to boost William's claim to the throne of England. Even if the embassy was not about William becoming king of England, it suggests close ties between England and Normandy.
- It was used by the Normans to portray Harold as an oath-breaker after Harold became king instead of helping William to the throne of England.

Key term

Hostages*

People given to another person as part of an oath or agreement. If the oath or agreement was broken, the hostages could be killed or maimed, e.g. have hands cut off, be blinded (or both).

Source A

A scene from the Bayeux Tapestry, probably produced in Kent around 1070 on the orders of Bishop Odo of Bayeux. This scene shows Harold swearing an oath in William's presence.

VBI hAROLD:SACRAMENTVM:FECIT: hIC hAROLD:DVX:
VVILLELMO DVCI:

| William, Duke of Normandy | Holy relics in a shrine | Harold Godwinson | Holy relics in a shrine | The text at the top says that Harold and William went to Bayeux, 'where Harold made an oath to Duke William'. |

The rising against Earl Tostig

Reasons for the rising

Tostig Godwinson became Earl of Northumbria in 1055 after the death of Earl Siward.

Earl Tostig ruled Northumbria for ten years. In October 1065, there was an uprising against Tostig, led by important Northumbrian thegns. There were several reasons for the rising: you can read about them in the map on this page.

The rising of 1065 began with rebels marching on York, the city from which Northumbria was governed. There, the rebels killed as many of Tostig's housecarls and servants as they could find, and declared Tostig an outlaw.

They invited Morcar, the brother of the Earl of Mercia, to be their earl instead of Tostig.

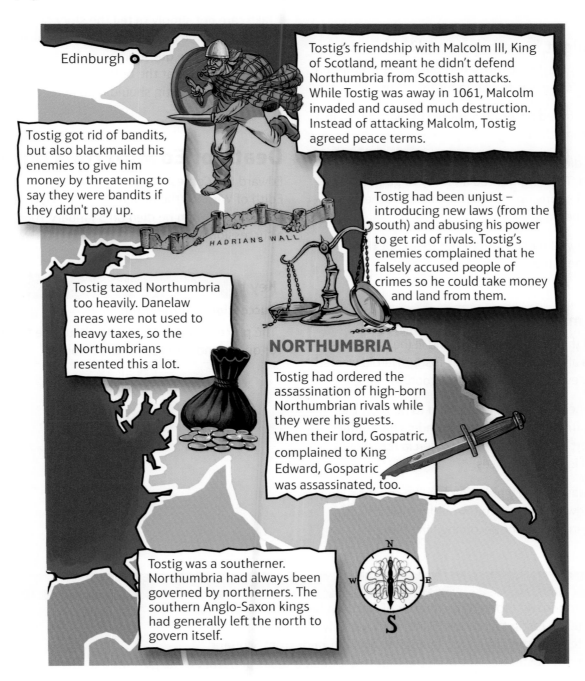

Edinburgh

Tostig's friendship with Malcolm III, King of Scotland, meant he didn't defend Northumbria from Scottish attacks. While Tostig was away in 1061, Malcolm invaded and caused much destruction. Instead of attacking Malcolm, Tostig agreed peace terms.

Tostig got rid of bandits, but also blackmailed his enemies to give him money by threatening to say they were bandits if they didn't pay up.

HADRIANS WALL

Tostig had been unjust – introducing new laws (from the south) and abusing his power to get rid of rivals. Tostig's enemies complained that he falsely accused people of crimes so he could take money and land from them.

Tostig taxed Northumbria too heavily. Danelaw areas were not used to heavy taxes, so the Northumbrians resented this a lot.

NORTHUMBRIA

Tostig had ordered the assassination of high-born Northumbrian rivals while they were his guests. When their lord, Gospatric, complained to King Edward, Gospatric was assassinated, too.

Tostig was a southerner. Northumbria had always been governed by northerners. The southern Anglo-Saxon kings had generally left the north to govern itself.

Harold's response to the rising

Instead of raising an army to march north and defeat the rebels, Harold instead met with them. He told them that King Edward agreed to their demands:

- Tostig would be exiled
- Morcar would be the new earl of Northumbria.

Harold married Morcar's sister to seal the deal. (Danelaw said a man could have two wives.) The rising had begun at the start of October 1065. By 1 November, Tostig was exiled.

What might have happened?

- Harold agreed that Tostig had pushed Northumbria too far: Tostig was to blame for the rising.

- Tostig accused his brother Harold of plotting against him, saying the rising was a plan to replace him.

- Harold did not actually do what King Edward ordered. The king wanted an army to go north and crush the uprising, but Harold and the other earls didn't obey.

- King Edward had no choice but to accept the rebels' demands.

Harold may have wanted the crown

- Edward the Confessor was old and ill (he died three months after the rising against Tostig). Harold wanted to show everyone he would be a good, fair king.

- Harold needed a united kingdom to hold off the threats from Normandy and Scandinavia: conflict with Northumbria (and maybe Mercia too) would weaken English defences.

- Tostig was probably planning how he could be king when Edward died. Harold would not want Tostig getting in the way of becoming king himself.

Exam-style question, Section B

Explain why there was a rising against Earl Tostig in 1065.

You may use the following in your answer:

- the Danelaw
- taxation.

You **must** also use information of your own. **12 marks**

Exam tip

Take care not simply to tell the story of the rebellion, which would be description. Instead, link each point you make to the question by giving a reason. The summary points at the bottom of this page about the rising against Tostig should help here.

Death of Edward the Confessor

Edward the Confessor had no children with his wife, Edith of Wessex (the daughter of Earl Godwin). This meant that, when he died on 5 January 1066, there was a succession* crisis.

Key term

Succession* (to the throne)

The process that decides who should be the next king or queen and 'succeed' to the throne.

Summary

- Short term: Tostig ordered the murder of Northumbrian aristocrats (Gospatric).
- Longer term: Tostig taxed Northumbria too heavily: people resented this.
- Longer term: Tostig did not do enough to prevent raids from Scotland.
- Longer term: Tostig was not from the Danelaw: Danelaw areas preferred to be governed by Danelaw aristocrats.

Source B

The death of Edward the Confessor, portrayed in the Bayeux Tapestry.

The Bayeux Tapestry shows the death of Edward at his palace in Westminster – a picture of this scene is on the next page. Edward is with a small circle of people:

Edith

Archbishop Stigand

Harold

This shows King Edward indicating that Harold should be the next king

- his wife Edith, who sits at his feet
- Stigand, the Anglo-Saxon Archbishop of Canterbury
- one of Edward's ministers
- Harold.

Edward is shown holding out his hand to Harold. Other sources report that Edward told Harold to protect the kingdom. Harold understood this to mean that he was to be king – Harold II.

1.2 The last years of Edward the Confessor and the succession crisis: summary

- The house of Godwin had become the real 'power behind the throne' in Anglo-Saxon England.
- Harold's embassy to Normandy and his decisions over Tostig had major consequences.
- Edward the Confessor died childless, causing a succession crisis.

Checkpoint

Strengthen

S1 When did: Harold become Earl of Wessex; Tostig get exiled; King Edward die?

S2 Describe two reasons why the Godwins made themselves so powerful.

Challenge

C1 In your own words, say why you think Harold went against King Edward's wishes over the rising against Tostig.

How confident do you feel about your answers to these questions? If you are not sure that you have answered them well, try the following study skills activity.

Activity ?

KWL is a strategy to help you take control of your own learning. It stands for Know – Want to know – Learned. This is how it works:

a Draw a table with three columns: 'Know', 'Want to know' and 'Learned'.

b For any topic you are learning about, write down what you know about it already.

c Next, write down what else you'd like know, what questions you have about what you know.

d When you find out the answers, write them in the 'Learned' column.

Use this method to make notes on this section. Here's an example:

Know	Want to know	Learned
Tostig was from Wessex; Northumbria was different.	Why was Northumbria different?	Part of Northumbria in Danelaw. Different laws, different language, tax lower.

1.3 The rival claimants for the throne

Learning outcomes

- Understand the rival claims to the kingdom following Edward's death.
- Understand the appointment and reign of Harold Godwinson.
- Understand the reasons for and significance of the battles of Gate Fulford and Stamford Bridge.

Harold Godwinson (c1022–1066)

Just before he died, King Edward said that Harold should be king after him: Harold had witnesses to prove this. He also had other good claims to the throne: he was King Edward's brother in law, his role in recent years as the king's right-hand man, his influence with the earls and thegns, and his record as a brilliant warrior.

Harold Godwinson	
Claim	Appointed as King Edward's successor by the king himself.
Strength of claim	Good – supported by witnesses, but ones loyal to Harold.
Chance of success	Excellent – Harold had the support required to be made king.

Edgar Aethling (c1051–c1126)

However, King Edward already had an heir: Edgar the Aethling. As Edward's nephew, Edgar was directly descended from royal blood. His title 'Aethling' meant a prince of royal blood. But in 1066, the leading men of Anglo-Saxon England, the Witan, knew the threats from Scandinavia and Normandy were very serious. They thought a teenage king was not the right choice in such troubled times.

Edgar Aethling	
Claim	Royal blood.
Strength of claim	Strong in theory, but he had no way to back it up.
Chance of success	Weak – although teenagers had become kings before, Anglo-Saxon England at this time needed a warrior-king to defend it against foreign threats.

King Edward himself said I should be king. The Witan agrees. Edward was my brother in law and I served as his deputy and adviser.

King Edward and I agreed I should be king of England. Harold Godwinson swore a sacred oath to me that I should be king.

There was a secret treaty that makes me the heir to England's throne. Tostig tells me England's Danelaw wants me as king!

King Edward was my uncle. I'm the only one here actually related to the old king. I'm his heir and I've got royal blood.

| Harold Godwinson | William of Normandy | Harald Hardrada | Edgar Aethling |

▶ The four claimants to the throne of Anglo-Saxon England.

Harald Hardrada (c1015–1066)

Harald Hardrada was the king of Norway. He was a fearsome old Viking warrior, feared across Europe. His nickname 'Hardrada' meant 'stern ruler'. His claim to the English throne was based on Viking secret deals and treaties.

After Tostig Godwinson was exiled from England he supported Hardrada. He told him that Harold was very unpopular in England, especially in the north.

Harald Hardrada	
Claim	Based on a secret deal about another secret deal made by other Vikings!
Strength of claim	Weak, although the Danelaw might welcome a Viking king.
Chance of success	Good, as Harald had perhaps 15,000 warriors and 300 or more Viking longships at his command (together with Tostig's 12 ships), all used to invade countries across the North Sea.

William of Normandy (c1028–1087)

William was Duke of Normandy, Normandy was a small country (smaller than Northumbria) surrounded by enemies. England offered the chance of real wealth and power for Wiliam.

William said Edward promised that William could be king after him in 1051. He also said Harold had agreed to this during his embassy to Normandy in 1064. The pope (leader of the Christian Church) believed William's claim. This proved very important in getting the support William needed for his invasion (see page 34).

Harold and the Witan clearly knew about William's claim. That is why Harold started getting ready for an invasion from Normandy as soon as King Edward died.

William of Normandy	
Claim	An agreement with King Edward.
Strength of claim	Good: the pope supported William's claim, though Harold and the Witan did not agree.
Chance of success	Quite good: the Normans were Europe's best warriors, but getting across the Channel was very risky.

Activity ?

Split into three groups: Group 1 are Anglo-Saxon actors performing 'The death of Edward the Confessor'; Group 2 is the court of Harald Hardrada; Group 3 is the court of William of Normandy.

a Group 1 needs to plan what their performance is going to show and what they're going to say, before performing it to Groups 2 and 3.

b Groups 2 and 3 need to explain their reactions to the performance to the other groups.

Ideas for Group 1

Start with a freeze frame based on the deathbed scene on page 25.

Each character could speak in turn, for example:

King Edward: I am sad that we did not have a child of our own, Edith. Harold, look after Edith and the kingdom, too.

Harold: Does that mean I'm king?

Give speaking roles to Stigand and Edith and the minister, too.

Harold's coronation and reign

Harold Godwinson's coronation (the ceremony where he was crowned king) took place the same day as Edward was buried: 6 January 1066. That was very fast (Edward had waited for months to be crowned). Everything about the way Harold became king shows him seizing his opportunity as fast as he could.

The Witan

In Anglo-Saxon England, a king's eldest child did not automatically become king when the old king died. Instead, the Witan met to agree who should be king.

Edward died on 5 January and the Witan met on the same day to elect Harold as king. It was probably the need to make preparations for England's defence from William that made the Witan willing to elect King Harold II as quickly as possible. When news of the coronation reached William, he was furious.

King Harold's challenges

- Challenges from other powerful Anglo-Saxon earls: especially Wessex's old rival, Mercia.
- The problem in the north: would Northumbria accept Tostig's brother as king?
- Tostig: Harold's brother was travelling around Europe looking for allies against Harold, as their father, Godwin, had done against King Edward.
- William of Normandy: reports that William was building an invasion fleet soon reached the king.

King Harold's responses

- Straight after his coronation, Harold went to York, the chief city of Northumbria. He met Witan members who had not been present in London, to make sure he had their support.
- Harold then gathered the largest army England had ever seen. This army was positioned along the south coast of England to defend against invasion. He also had a large fleet on the south coast. Both the army and the fleet were levied (raised) from the fyrd.

Tostig sailed a fleet over to England in May 1066. But when he learned about the extraordinary strength of Harold's defences, Tostig left quickly and sailed round the coast to Lincoln. There a fight with the Mercians left Tostig with only 12 ships. He fled for Scotland, and then began plotting with Harald Hardrada in Norway.

Harold's army and fleet guarded the southern coast all summer. Harold had to keep his army and fleet supplied with food and drink: an expensive and complicated business. But the expected Norman invasion did not come. By September, it was time to stand down the army and fleet.

Summary

Harold acted very quickly to get ready for William's invasion.

- He made sure all the important men in England supported him.
- He got together a very large army and fleet.
- His defences in the south were very strong: they frightened off Tostig's fleet.

The battles of Gate Fulford and Stamford Bridge

Timeline

Gate Fulford and Stamford Bridge, 1066

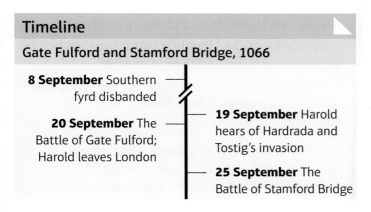

8 September Southern fyrd disbanded

20 September The Battle of Gate Fulford; Harold leaves London

19 September Harold hears of Hardrada and Tostig's invasion

25 September The Battle of Stamford Bridge

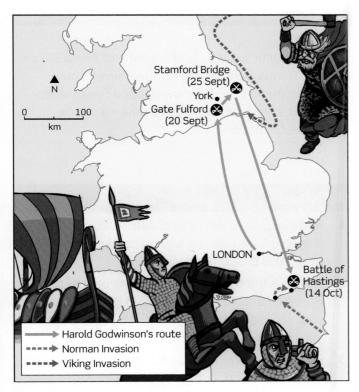

Figure 1.6 Map showing Harold's march north and return south to face invasion of William of Normandy.

In September 1066, Harald Hardrada and Tostig attacked. Hardrada's fleet numbered around 200–300 warships, carrying perhaps 10,000 Vikings. Landing at the River Humber, they marched up to York – once a Viking city. They met an army led by Morcar and his elder brother Edwin (the earls of Northumbria and Mercia) at Gate Fulford. The brothers could have stayed behind the strongly defended walls of York. Instead they fought a battle against the huge Viking army.

Gate Fulford (20 September 1066)

Gate Fulford was a crushing defeat for Edwin and Morcar. There were a number of military reasons for this outcome:

- Edwin and Morcar were probably outnumbered: it is thought they had 6,000 troops against perhaps 9,000 for Hardrada and Tostig (we know some thousands stayed with the ships).
- Hardrada and his housecarls were battle-hardened veterans, and he used a clever strategy in the battle. He placed Tostig's weaker troops on one wing and, when the English rushed at them, he was able to hit them with his best troops from the side.
- Edwin and Morcar stationed their army with marshland at their backs. This meant their troops had nowhere to go when they were pushed back.

The English army tried to run away into the marsh, but they got stuck in the swampy ground and were slaughtered.

King Harold's march north

Learning of the invasion (possibly by beacon signals*), Harold took his housecarls north, travelling 185 miles in five days. This was an incredible military achievement. When he set out, he did not yet know about Gate Fulford.

Key term

Beacon signals*

Fires lit along a chain of high places (cliffs, hill tops) to signal over long distances that an invasion had occurred.

Harold must have been confident that it was now too late in the year for William to cross the Channel.

- The English Channel often has bad storms in autumn.
- The wind was still blowing from the north when Harold set off. He knew this would stop William's ships from sailing.
- Harold knew William would have found it difficult to keep his army waiting once summer was over. Keeping armies supplied with food and drink was very expensive.

After the Battle of Gate Fulford, the city of York had surrendered to Hardrada and Tostig. Hardrada and Tostig were told that hostages from York would be handed over to them at a place called Stamford Bridge.

Stamford Bridge (25 September 1066)

King Harold had probably learned of the hostage deal as he travelled towards York, and decided on his strategy.

- There was a small hill overlooking Stamford Bridge, which meant that his army could approach undetected.
- The battle was a complete success for Harold: Hardrada and Tostig were both killed, probably with many thousands of their men.
- It is reported that only 24 of Hardrada's longships returned to Norway, out of the 200 or more that had sailed in August.

▶ William crossing the Channel, as shown in the Bayeux Tapestry.

Harold's victory was helped by several military factors:

- The Viking army had their weapons and shields with them, but had left their armour on their ships (it was a hot day) as well as perhaps a third of their men.
- Harold took Hardrada and Tostig by surprise.
- Hardrada's army had fought a battle five days before and were not expecting to fight another.
- Harold's housecarls eventually broke the Viking shield wall*. This shows that Harold's men must have been awesome warriors.

Harold had secured his kingdom against a very significant threat. However, news soon reached him that William had landed on the south coast after all, on 28 September. Harold set off south to fight the third and most significant battle of 1066.

Key term

Shield wall*

A military tactic used by both Viking and Anglo-Saxon armies. Troops were set out in a line, several men deep. The men at the front overlapped their shields, with their spears sticking out, to create a strong defensive formation.

Activities

1 As a class, recreate a shield wall. PE equipment works well for this. Is it a good defence? How might you break it?

2 List your top three reasons why Harold beat Hardrada and Tostig at Stamford Bridge. Compare your choices with a partner: do you agree? Have you changed your mind?

3 Imagine you are Harold, deciding how to respond to Hardrada and Tostig's invasion. Draw up a pros and cons list for staying put in Wessex.

Were the battles significant?

What happened at the battles had a big impact on the Battle of Hastings. But how significant were these?

Significant because…	However…
Hardrada and Tostig's invasion meant that Harold was not in the south to prevent William's invasion.	Harold had already disbanded the southern fyrd in September anyway, as its time was up.
Fighting at Stamford Bridge then marching south again to fight William must have exhausted Harold and his housecarls. This must have played a part in the Battle of Hastings.	Harold and his housecarls had just won a victory against the famous warrior Harald Hardrada. Morale must have been high.
Harold's success at taking Hardrada by surprise might have made him over-confident. Instead of waiting for William in fortified London, he rushed to do battle, with fatal consequences.	Harold and the Witan had been waiting and preparing for William for months, perhaps years. A battle on the south coast, on Harold's home turf, may have seemed the best chance of victory.

Activity **?**

Concept maps (spider diagrams) are ideal for working out the links between factors and between topics. You can build up a concept map of a topic in three main stages:

a Put your topic (or issue or question) in the middle of a big piece of paper.

b Draw out 'branches' from the central topic to important categories of the topic.

c From those, draw out 'sub-branches' to individual facts or ideas that connect to them.

It is a good idea to colour-code your different categories and add images to make your map memorable.

Try putting together a concept map on 'Harold's problems in 1066'.

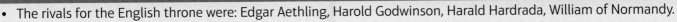

1.3 The rival claimants for the throne: summary

- The rivals for the English throne were: Edgar Aethling, Harold Godwinson, Harald Hardrada, William of Normandy.
- Harold Godwinson acted quickly to claim the throne, with the Witan's support.
- Harold's preparations for the expected Norman invasion were thorough.
- Harald and Tostig's northern invasion was defeated, but had serious consequences for the Battle of Hastings.

Checkpoint

Strengthen

S1 Describe the claim to the throne of two of the rival claimants.

S2 Give one reason that helps explain the outcomes of **a)** the Battle of Gate Fulford and **b)** the Battle of Stamford Bridge.

Challenge

C1 In your own words, summarise the significance of the Battle of Stamford Bridge – why it was important.

How confident do you feel about your answers to these questions? If you're not sure you have answered them well, try the above study skills activity.

1.4 The Norman invasion

Learning outcomes

- Understand the events of the Battle of Hastings.
- Understand the reasons for William's victory.

Timeline

The Norman invasion, 1066

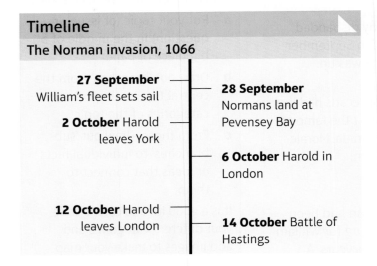

27 September William's fleet sets sail

28 September Normans land at Pevensey Bay

2 October Harold leaves York

6 October Harold in London

12 October Harold leaves London

14 October Battle of Hastings

Activity ?

Go online and find a site featuring the whole Bayeux Tapestry. Pick one scene from the Battle of Hastings you like and print it onto A4 paper. Add a caption and labels to the image that include the following information:

a What part of the battle it is showing.

b Who you think the Normans are and who you think the English are (hint: moustaches).

c Looking at the scene you have chosen, what do you think it was like to be in the battle?

The Battle of Hastings (14 October 1066)

Although we do not know everything about the Battle of Hastings, we do know some important facts about it.

1. Harold did not manage a surprise attack

Harold rushed down to Hastings from London to try and surprise William. But William's scouts found out about Harold's advance. The Norman army arrived while Harold's army was gathering together on a wooded hilltop. Both sides rushed to get control of the high ground of the battlefield. Harold got there first and organised his shield wall along a ridge.

2. William sent his foot soldiers in first

The battle lasted eight hours: very long for a medieval battle. William first sent his archers forward, but the English caught the arrows on their shields. The shield wall held off the Norman foot soldiers. The Norman cavalry then charged up the hill, but failed to break the wall. The battle started in Harold's favour.

3. William showed his face

Norman attacks continued throughout the day, with the Anglo-Saxon shield wall standing firm. At one point, a rumour went round William's army that he had been killed. William tipped his helmet back to show he was still alive. This stopped his troops from panicking and running away.

4. Harold's shield wall began to break up

After one Norman attack, part of Harold's army left the shield wall to chase William's men down the hill. They were trapped at the bottom of the hill and killed. The Saxon shield wall began to break up. This made it harder to defend against Norman cavalry charges.

5. The last stand

Harold, his brothers, housecarls and remaining men held their ground. But they were now heavily outnumbered. They could not hold off the Norman cavalry charges. Harold and his brothers were killed. William had won.

Elite troops: knights and housecarls

Elite troops are the members of an army that have received special training to fight in a particular way, and have specialist equipment.

William's knights

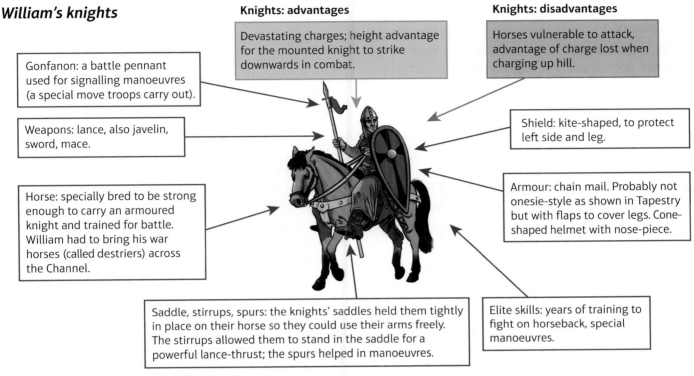

Knights: advantages

Devastating charges; height advantage for the mounted knight to strike downwards in combat.

Knights: disadvantages

Horses vulnerable to attack, advantage of charge lost when charging up hill.

Gonfanon: a battle pennant used for signalling manoeuvres (a special move troops carry out).

Weapons: lance, also javelin, sword, mace.

Horse: specially bred to be strong enough to carry an armoured knight and trained for battle. William had to bring his war horses (called destriers) across the Channel.

Shield: kite-shaped, to protect left side and leg.

Armour: chain mail. Probably not onesie-style as shown in Tapestry but with flaps to cover legs. Cone-shaped helmet with nose-piece.

Saddle, stirrups, spurs: the knights' saddles held them tightly in place on their horse so they could use their arms freely. The stirrups allowed them to stand in the saddle for a powerful lance-thrust; the spurs helped in manoeuvres.

Elite skills: years of training to fight on horseback, special manoeuvres.

Figure 1.7 Features of Norman knights.

Harold's housecarls

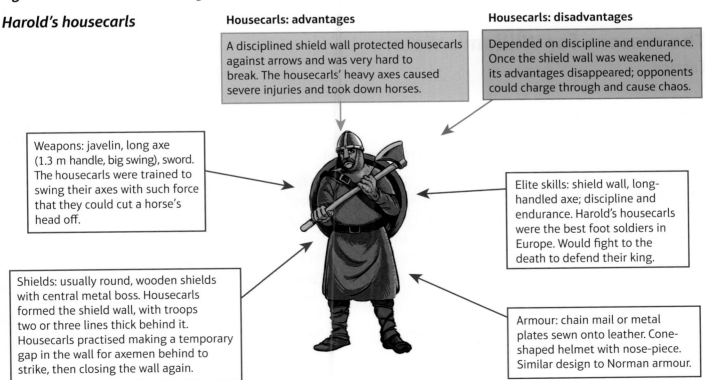

Housecarls: advantages

A disciplined shield wall protected housecarls against arrows and was very hard to break. The housecarls' heavy axes caused severe injuries and took down horses.

Housecarls: disadvantages

Depended on discipline and endurance. Once the shield wall was weakened, its advantages disappeared; opponents could charge through and cause chaos.

Weapons: javelin, long axe (1.3 m handle, big swing), sword. The housecarls were trained to swing their axes with such force that they could cut a horse's head off.

Shields: usually round, wooden shields with central metal boss. Housecarls formed the shield wall, with troops two or three lines thick behind it. Housecarls practised making a temporary gap in the wall for axemen behind to strike, then closing the wall again.

Elite skills: shield wall, long-handled axe; discipline and endurance. Harold's housecarls were the best foot soldiers in Europe. Would fight to the death to defend their king.

Armour: chain mail or metal plates sewn onto leather. Cone-shaped helmet with nose-piece. Similar design to Norman armour.

Figure 1.8 Features of Anglo-Saxon housecarls.

Other troops

Both armies had elite troops, but most of each army was made up of ordinary soldiers.

- William had perhaps 800 knights and 4,000–6,000 foot soldiers.
- Harold may have had 6,000–7,000 men in his army in total (we don't know how many housecarls he had).
- The two armies may have been similar in size, though historians cannot be sure.

Harold's fyrdsmen

Harold's ordinary soldiers were men who he had hastily levied (taken) from the fyrd on his trip south.

- Not all these levies turned up in time. Harold decided to take on William without them.
- The thegns had good weapons, shields and armour. The general fyrd may only have had farming tools to fight with.
- There were not many Anglo-Saxon archers at the Battle of Hastings – they may have been amongst the troops that did not turn up in time.

The reasons for William's victory
Tactics

Harold's tactics

Because Harold lost the Battle of Hastings, it is tempting to argue his shield-wall tactics were wrong. Is this fair?

There are arguments in favour of the shield wall:

- Shield walls work well against archers. At first, William's archers had little impact on Harold's army because the shield wall caught the arrows on their shields.
- Early on in the battle, the shield wall also proved effective against the Norman cavalry. Because the horses had to charge up hill, they didn't hit the wall fast enough or hard enough. The housecarls' huge battle axes could chop the horses down.

Exam-style question, Section B

Describe **two** features of William's troops at the Battle of Hastings. **4 marks**

Exam tip

Make sure both the features you use are relevant – don't describe features of Harold's troops by mistake! Make sure you add supporting information to both.

William's foot soldiers

- These were a mixture of Normans and hired soldiers from all over Europe.
- Most were probably not trained to work together with the Norman knights in battle.
- Some of the foot soldiers were archers and crossbowmen.
- Most Norman archers had padded jackets as armour (called gambesons).
- The others would have been 'heavy' footsoldiers, with chain mail armour, shields and javelins or swords.

William's tactics

William used different attacking tactics until he found what worked.

- At first, his archers didn't have much effect on the shield wall: they had to shoot up hill while staying out of the shield wall's javelin range. But, once the wall started to break up, the archers could get closer and cause more damage.
- Cavalry were usually only used against enemy cavalry or to chase down retreating foot soldiers, but William used them against the shield wall. At first, the tactic didn't work but, once the shield wall had been weakened, the mounted knights could charge through and break it up.

Source A

A scene from the Bayeux Tapestry showing the Anglo-Saxon shield wall facing a Norman cavalry charge.

Shield wall – but broken up and vulnerable

Arrows caught on shields

A housecarl stepping through the shield wall to swing his axe

Lances – all raised together

No armour for horses – vulnerable to axes

Long shields cover the knights' sides

This group has gathered around a standard (battle flag)

Dead troops scattered on the ground. These could be Normans (no moustaches)

Stirrups allow the knights to stand and make a powerful lance thrust

A decapitated Norman

What weakened the shield wall?

The most important factor in William's victory was the weakening of the shield wall. This probably happened when Harold's foot soldiers (the general fyrd) chased after Normans who were running away because they wanted to grab abandoned weapons, armour and horses.

This could have been a special Norman tactic, called a 'feigned retreat' ('feigned means 'fake'). Normans had used this tactic before in battles against the French. Some of their troops would pretend to run away in panic, hoping that the other side would chase after them. Then the Normans would turn round, surround their opponents, and kill them. It was risky because a feigned retreat could very easily turn into a real one. It took a lot of skill and training to make the feigned retreat tactic work.

Activities   ?

1 Describe one strength and one weakness of
   a) William's troops and **b)** Harold's troops.

2 Give one reason why William's tactics helped him win the Battle of Hastings.

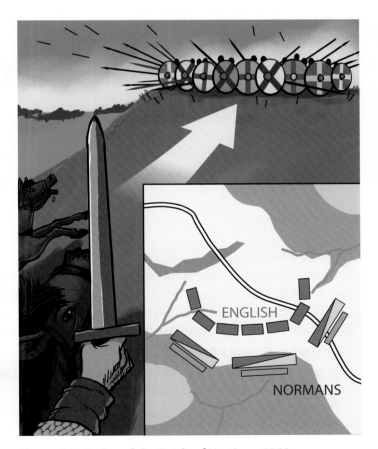

Figure 1.9 A plan of the Battle of Hastings, 1066.

Leadership

William's leadership

He was ruthless: He let his men cause a lot of damage in the area, burning houses and stealing food. This meant Harold couldn't use any of it.

He waited: He knew Harold would eventually need to disband the fyrd. He could then take Harold by surprise.

He was lucky: When he sailed, he was lucky to escape the storms.

William's leadership

He was organised: As soon as the troops landed, he marched to Hastings and built a 'prefabricated' castle – this meant it was prepared in sections and could be quickly put together. This gave him a secure base.

He was ambitious: Crossing the channel with horses had never been done before. His knights needed their trained horses. Special boats with flat bottoms were built.

He kept his army together: He needed to be strong to do this. Armies need lots of food and water, but William kept them under control and stopped them stealing from Norman farmers.

Summary

William's leadership
- Keeping his large army waiting until the autumn, crossing the Channel during a storm and transporting horses across the Channel were all very risky and difficult.
- William's successful invasion shows he was a brilliant leader: everything was well organised and he was clearly working to a detailed plan.

Harold's leadership

Harold's decision	Why did Harold make that decision?
The sources suggest that Harold waited for perhaps five days in London before continuing to Hastings. He waited there to gather troops. London was well-fortified and Harold could have waited there for William to attack. Instead, Harold rushed down to Hastings.	• Taking an invading army by surprise had worked brilliantly against Harald and Tostig: it was worth trying again. • If Harold waited in London, there was a good chance that William would get reinforcements from Normandy. • Anglo-Saxons were no good at defending towns against sieges. William was highly experienced at sieges. • Harold was angry at the destruction in Wessex and wanted to stop it.
Criticisms of Harold's decision	
• In getting down to William as soon as possible, Harold weakened his chances of success because he did not have as many troops as he could have had. • He didn't manage to take William by surprise.	

Harold's leadership

At the time, Harold may have done what he did for very good reasons. However:

- Calling out his southern army in May was a problem as he then had to feed and house it for four months, before finally disbanding it.
- Deciding to rush down to fight William in the south was not Harold's only option. He could have waited for William to come to him, in London.
- Harold had planned to surprise William, but it turned out the other way around. William arrived before Harold's army were ready.

Summary

Harold's leadership

- Harold's decision to rush down to Hastings does not look like good leadership.
- William guessed what Harold's plans would be and he took advantage of this.

Leadership and luck

In the chaos of battle, anything could happen. For example, Harold being hit in the eye by an arrow. Both Normans and Anglo-Saxons believed God's will decided the result of battles: this could also be called luck.

Luck (or God's will) did play a large part in William's victory: but Harold could also have won. For example:

- Harald Hardrada's invasion happening when it did was very bad luck for Harold. The defeat at Gate Fulford and Harold's fast march up to York and down again weakened Harold's defences.
- William decided to sail for England after winter storms began in the Channel. His fleet was very lucky not to have been destroyed.
- Medieval battles were chaotic – the Bayeux Tapestry shows Odo of Bayeux (William's half-brother), for example, having to encourage young Norman knights who were panicking. Despite all his planning and tactics, William was also very lucky not to have lost.

Activity ?

There's a thinking skills technique called 'Plus – Minus – Interesting' that is a useful tool for analysis and helps with recalling information, too.

a Plus – write a strength or an advantage of the feature you are studying (e.g. Norman troops).
b Minus – write a weakness or limitation of the feature.
c Interesting – write something you find interesting about the feature.

Try this for the topics in this section: it's especially good for comparing troops, tactics and leadership.

1.4 The Norman invasion: summary

- The Norman invasion was timed to follow Harold's disbanding of the fyrd.
- An attack late in the year was very risky due to storms in the Channel.
- The Battle of Hastings lasted all day, suggesting the two armies were evenly matched.
- William's victory at the Battle of Hastings has many interlinking causes.

Checkpoint

Strengthen

S1 Describe two features of William's troops.
S2 Describe two features of Harold's troops.
S3 Outline the different stages of the Battle of Hastings.

Challenge

C1 Why do you think Harold lost the Battle of Hastings? Give at least two reasons.
C2 Why do you think William won the Battle of Hastings? Give at least two reasons.

How confident do you feel about your answers to these questions? If you are not sure you have answered them well, try the above activity.

THINKING HISTORICALLY — Cause and Consequence (3a&b)

1 Work in pairs.

Describe to your partner a situation where things did not work out as you planned. Then explain how you would have done things differently to get the result you wanted. Your partner will then tell the group about that situation and whether they think the changes you would make would make a difference.

2 Work individually.

The first battle of 1066 was Gate Fulford, when the army of Earls Edwin and Morcar attempted to defend the North against invasion by Harald Hardrada.

    a Write down what Morcar hoped to achieve at Gate Fulford.

    b Write down what Morcar did – his actions.

    c Write down what the outcome was: what happened at Gate Fulford?

    d In what ways do the outcomes not live up to Morcar's expectations?

3 Think about King Harold and Harald Hardrada's invasion attempt.

    a Write down what you think King Harold's aims were in September 1066. What actions did he take? What were the consequences?

    b In what ways were the consequences of Hardrada's invasion not anticipated by King Harold?

    c In what ways did Hardrada's invasion turn out better for King Harold (in the short-term) than he might have expected?

Exam-style question, Section B

Explain why there was a succession crisis after the death of Edward the Confessor.

You may use the following in your answer:

- Normandy
- the Witan.

You **must** also use information of your own. **12 marks**

Exam tip

For this answer, you need to identify the features of the succession crisis, then develop evidence to support each point.

Here are some sentence starters to help you get going.

- Edward the Confessor died without having any children. This caused a succession crisis because…
- Edward had a nephew, Edgar, who could have been his heir. But the Witan chose Harold. This added to the crisis because…
- William of Normandy believed he had a right to the throne of England because…
- Harold's brother Tostig added to the succession crisis because he told Harald Hardrada that…

Recap: Anglo-Saxon England and the Norman Conquest, 1060–66

Recall quiz

1. Who was the king of England before Harold?
2. Where was Harald Hardrada king of?
3. Name three of Harold Godwinson's brothers.
4. What was a burh?
5. What was the Anglo-Saxon name for a local lord (he lived in a manor house with a tower)?
6. List the four main claimants to the English throne after Edward died in January 1066.
7. Who won at Gate Fulford?
8. Who won at Stamford Bridge?
9. Name a tactic used by William at the Battle of Hastings.
10. Two of Harold's brothers died with him at the Battle of Hastings. What were their names and where were they earls of?

Source A

An Anglo-Saxon poem about a great English battle against the Vikings, has a thegn saying:

I give you my word that I will not retreat
One inch; I shall forge on
And avenge my lord in battle.
Now that he has fallen in the fight

Exam-style question, Section B

'The main reason for the English defeat at the Battle of Hastings was superior Norman tactics.'

How far do you agree? Explain your answer.

You may use the following in your answer:

- the 'feigned retreat'
- the shield wall.

You **must** also use information of your own.   **16 marks**

Exam tip

Remember that 'How far do you agree?' means you need to consider points that support the statement and points that support other causes.

- You could use the first bullet point to support the statement: 'The feigned retreat was a Norman tactic that weakened the shield wall…'
- The second bullet point could be used to argue against the statement: 'The shield wall was not disciplined enough…'

Remember to add a third point of your own, for example you could talk about leadership or luck.

Activities

1. Anglo-Saxons wrote epic poetry about bravery in battle and the honour of dying for their lord. Write a poem of your own, expressing the feelings of an Anglo-Saxon thegn who fought with Harold at the Battle of Hastings. Make it as epic as possible.
2. Put together a news-style report on the contenders for the throne of England following Edward's death in January 1066. Role-play interviews with the main contenders.
3. Draw a big concept map (spider diagram) for the topic: Reasons for William's victory. You will need to decide on some categories for your diagram – for example, tactics, luck, leadership, troops. Use A3 paper and colour-code your categories to help make them more memorable.

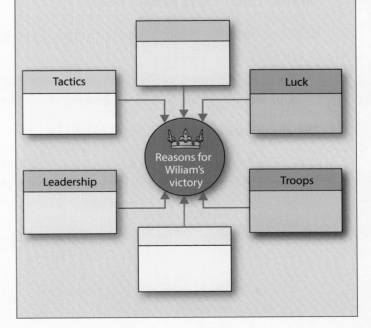

Writing historically: managing sentences

Successful historical writing is clearly expressed, using carefully managed sentence structures.

Learning outcomes

By the end of this lesson, you will understand how to:

- select and use single clause and multiple clause sentences.

Definitions

Clause: a group of words or unit of meaning that contains a verb (a 'doing' word, that describes an action) and can form part or all of a sentence, e.g. 'William I conquered the Anglo-Saxons'.

Single clause sentence: a sentence containing just one clause, e.g. 'William I conquered the Anglo-Saxons.'

Multiple clause sentence: a sentence containing two or more clauses, often linked with a conjunction, e.g. 'William I conquered the Anglo-Saxons and ruled England for 21 years'.

Co-ordinating conjunction: a word used to link two clauses of equal importance within a sentence, e.g. 'and', 'but', 'so', 'or', etc.

How can I structure my sentences clearly?

When you are explaining complicated events and ideas, you can end up writing very long sentences. These can make your writing difficult for the reader to follow.

Look at the extract below from a response to this exam-style question:

> Describe **two** features of the social system of Anglo–Saxon England. **(4 marks)**

> Someone's position in Anglo-Saxon society depended on how much land they owned but the thegns who were the local lords could lose their land and become peasants or slaves and free farmers could rise to become thegns.

1. The writer of the response above has linked every piece of information in their answer into one, very long sentence.

How many different pieces of information has the writer included in this answer? Re-write each piece of information as a **single clause sentence**. For example:

> The thegns were local lords.

2. Look again at your answer to Question 1. Which of the single clause sentences would you link together? Rewrite the response twice, experimenting with linking different sentences together using **conjunctions** such as 'and', 'but' or 'so'. Remember: you are aiming to make your writing as clear and precise as possible.

How can I use conjunctions to link my ideas?

There are several types of **multiple clause sentence** structures you can use to link your ideas.

If you want to balance or contrast two ideas of equal importance within a sentence, you can use co-ordinating conjunctions to link them.

Look at the extract below from a response to this exam-style question:

> Explain why William won the Battle of Hastings. **(12 marks)**

> William's leadership was a key reason for his success. He waited for Harold to disband the fyrd and kept his forces together and sailed as soon as he heard. This not only weakened Harold's forces but also took Harold by surprise. In the end he won not through tactics but because the Saxons were unprepared and rushing from fighting the Vikings.

These co-ordinating conjunctions link equally important actions that happened at the same time.

These paired co-ordinating conjunctions contrast two possible causes.

These paired co-ordinating conjunctions link and balance two equally important ideas.

   3. Experiment with rewriting some or all of the response, using different sentence structures and different ways of linking ideas.

Improving an answer

   4. Now look at the final paragraph below, which shows the response to the exam-style question above.

> William's patience and leadership gave him an advantage. William's preparations were thorough. Harold's position was growing weaker. Many of the Anglo-Saxon warriors had fought and marched already. The Anglo-Saxons were exhausted. William's tactics were clever. His varied tactics took advantage of the luck he had.

   Rewrite this paragraph, choosing some conjunctions from the Co-ordinating Conjunction Bank below to link, balance or contrast the writer's ideas.

Co-ordinating Conjunction Bank	
and	not only… but also…
but	either… or…
or	neither… nor…
so	both… and…

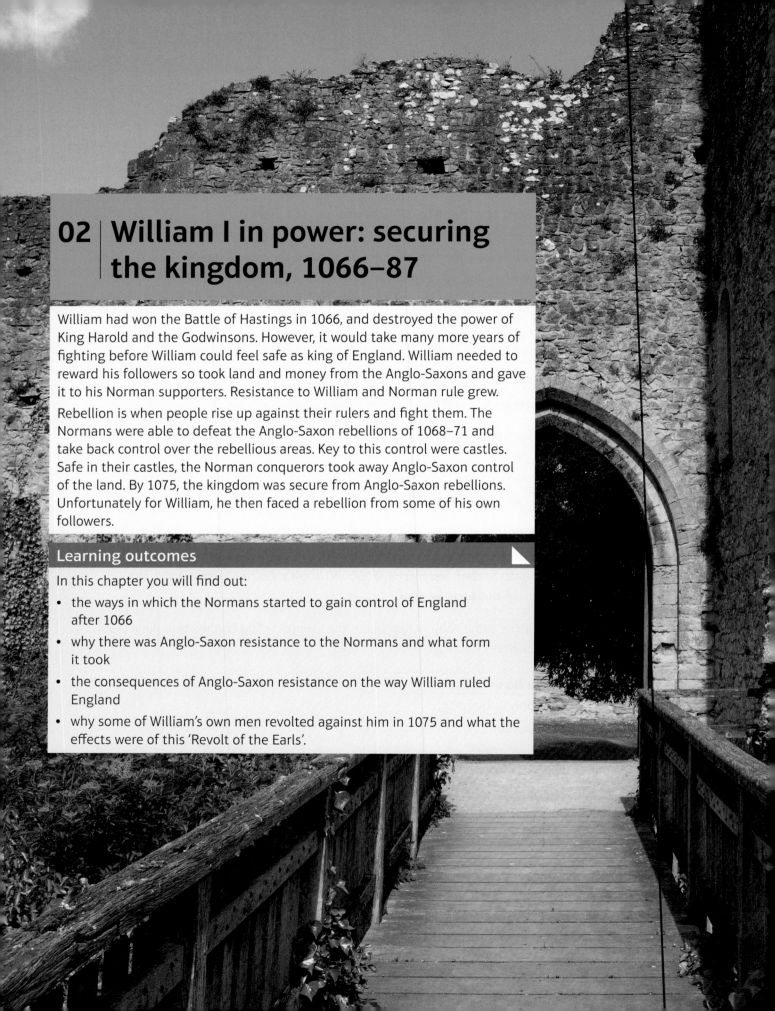

02 | William I in power: securing the kingdom, 1066–87

William had won the Battle of Hastings in 1066, and destroyed the power of King Harold and the Godwinsons. However, it would take many more years of fighting before William could feel safe as king of England. William needed to reward his followers so took land and money from the Anglo-Saxons and gave it to his Norman supporters. Resistance to William and Norman rule grew.

Rebellion is when people rise up against their rulers and fight them. The Normans were able to defeat the Anglo-Saxon rebellions of 1068–71 and take back control over the rebellious areas. Key to this control were castles. Safe in their castles, the Norman conquerors took away Anglo-Saxon control of the land. By 1075, the kingdom was secure from Anglo-Saxon rebellions. Unfortunately for William, he then faced a rebellion from some of his own followers.

Learning outcomes

In this chapter you will find out:

- the ways in which the Normans started to gain control of England after 1066
- why there was Anglo-Saxon resistance to the Normans and what form it took
- the consequences of Anglo-Saxon resistance on the way William ruled England
- why some of William's own men revolted against him in 1075 and what the effects were of this 'Revolt of the Earls'.

The submission of the earls, 1066

What happened after the Battle of Hastings?

William and his army returned to Hastings after the battle. He waited there to see if the Anglo-Saxon nobles would come and surrender to him as the new king of England. No one came.

Anglo-Saxons retreat to London

- Survivors from Harold's army fled back to London.
- The Witan elected Edgar Aethling as king.
- Stigand, Archbishop of Canterbury, and Ealdred, Archbishop of York, were involved in making Edgar king.
- Earl Edwin and Earl Morcar also supported Edgar.
- London may have been ready to fight William.

Normans control the south coast

- William got the south coast of England under his control. This was so reinforcements and supplies could be brought over from Normandy.
- William sent troops to capture Winchester, where England's royal treasury* was held.
- When William and his troops reached Dover, many became very ill, including William.
- If the Anglo-Saxons had attacked at this point, it is likely that William would have been defeated.

The march on London

William led his troops on a march to London. This was to force the Anglo-Saxons to accept him as king.

As they went, the Normans destroyed homes and farms. This was the same 'laying waste' that William had done around Hastings at the start of the invasion.

Frightened, the people of the towns on the way to London surrendered to William.

London was a city with strong stone walls, and did not surrender. Instead of attacking it directly, William led his troops west, continuing their path of destruction, until they reached Berkhamstead (see Figure 2.1).

The submission* at Berkhamstead

When William reached Berkhamstead, he was met by Edgar Aethling, together with leading men of London, Archbishop Ealdred and both Edwin and Morcar.

- They all submitted to William, swore oaths to obey him and gave him hostages to guarantee their promises.
- They offered him the crown of England.
- In return, William promised to be a 'gracious* lord' to them.

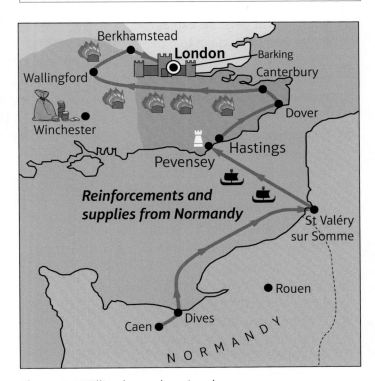

Figure 2.1 William's march on London.

Summary

William waits at Hastings for an Anglo-Saxon surrender. No one comes.

▼

The Witan elects Edgar Aethling as king.

▼

William's troops start taking control of Winchester and the south coast.

▼

At Hastings, William and his troops become very ill.

▼

William and his army march on London, 'laying waste' as they go.

▼

Edgar Aethling and the Anglo-Saxon earls submit to William at Berkhamstead.

Activities ?

1 Look back at page 26. Explain Edgar Aethling's claim to the throne of England. You could do this as a poster to encourage people to support him as king.

2 Using the table to help you, role-play a discussion between Edgar, Edwin, Morcar and Archbishop Ealdred about whether they should fight, sit out a siege of London or submit to William.

3 At the submission of the earls, William promised to be a 'gracious lord'. Using page 11 to help you, identify three things that an Anglo-Saxon earl would expect a 'gracious lord' to do.

Why did the earls submit in 1066?

The earls clearly felt that submission was better than fighting. It is true that their position had significant weaknesses as well as strengths, while the Normans had some key strengths as well as weaknesses.

Strengths of the earls' position	Weaknesses of William's position 
London was strongly **fortified** and William would lose a lot of men if he attacked it directly.	William and his troops were deep into enemy territory with no safe place to retreat to.
The earls and other leading noblemen supported Edgar, who had a much better claim to the throne than William.	William's claim to the throne didn't matter if the **Witan** had already chosen a new king: Edgar Aethling.
Edwin and Morcar controlled Mercia and Northumbria – half of England.	William's troops may have been **reinforced** from Normandy, but the numbers in his army were tiny (possibly 5,000) compared to what the Anglo-Saxon earls could gather.
Weaknesses of the earls' position	**Strengths of William's position**
Although London was strongly defended, William's route threatened to cut it off from reinforcements. He may also have spotted weaknesses in the defences.	William acted quickly to capture Winchester. That gave him control of the **royal treasury**. Without his treasury, Edgar could not reward followers, while William could.
Edgar took no decisive action as king, probably because the earls and he couldn't agree on what to do.	William was an extremely **effective** leader. His followers continued to obey him despite all the dangers.
The Battle of Hastings had been a crushing defeat. The best warriors in England had been killed.	Destroying everything in the path of his army was a **brutal but successful** plan for William that did not need huge troop numbers. People submitted to William rather than lose everything.

Rewarding followers and establishing control on the borderlands

On 25 December 1066, William was crowned king of England by Archbishop Ealdred in Westminster Abbey. At his coronation, William swore an oath that he would rule England like the best Anglo-Saxon kings had, if the English people would be loyal to him.

Source A

This extract from the Anglo-Saxon Chronicle's entry for 1066 describes William's coronation.

[A]nd William gave a pledge on the Gospels, and swore an oath besides, before [Archbishop] Ealdred would place the crown on his head, that he would govern this nation according to the best practice of his predecessors if they would be loyal to him. Nevertheless he imposed a very heavy tax on the country, and went oversea to Normandy in the spring.

Rewarding Anglo-Saxon loyalty

William wanted a trouble-free takeover, with Anglo-Saxons continuing to have important roles in government.

- Earls like Edwin and Morcar kept their earldoms.
- Archbishops like Stigand and Ealdred kept their positions.
- A Northumbrian lord, Gospatric, was made Earl of northern Northumbria (after paying William a large amount of money).
- William offered rewards for Anglo-Saxon loyalty. For example, he promised that Earl Edwin could marry William's daughter. This would have made Edwin very powerful in the new kingdom if it had happened.

Rewarding William's followers

But there was a problem. William also needed to reward his own followers. He had convinced people to join his invasion by promising them land. He had hired mercenaries* from all along the coast of north-west Europe by promising them money.

William rewarded his followers in three ways:

He sent **rich gifts** to the pope and to Church supporters in Normandy.

He set a **geld tax**. The tax was described as being 'very heavy' (see Source A). This brought in money to pay his mercenaries.

William I

He declared that, as king, all the **land** in England now belonged to him. He could give this land to anyone he wanted.

William said everyone who had fought against him at Hastings had lost the right to their lands. This gave him all the lands of the Godwinsons, for example, including Wessex, the richest earldom of all.

As king, Harold had also inherited all the royal estates from Edward. William kept much of this land for himself.

The biggest winners of William's followers were his family and closest advisers, almost all of whom were Normans. None of them were Anglo-Saxons. For example William made his half-brother Odo, a Bishop, the Earl of Kent.

Key term

Mercenaries*

Soldiers who fight for whoever is paying them rather than out of loyalty to a king or a country.

Establishing control on the borderlands

Wales had been a threat to Edward the Confessor's rule and William wanted the border between England and Wales to be made secure. Previous Anglo-Saxon kings had built their own defences along the borderland with Wales (called the March* of Wales).

William created three new earldoms centred on Hereford, Shrewsbury and Chester. These were called the Marcher earldoms.

> ### Key term
>
> **March***
>
> An Anglo-Saxon term for border.

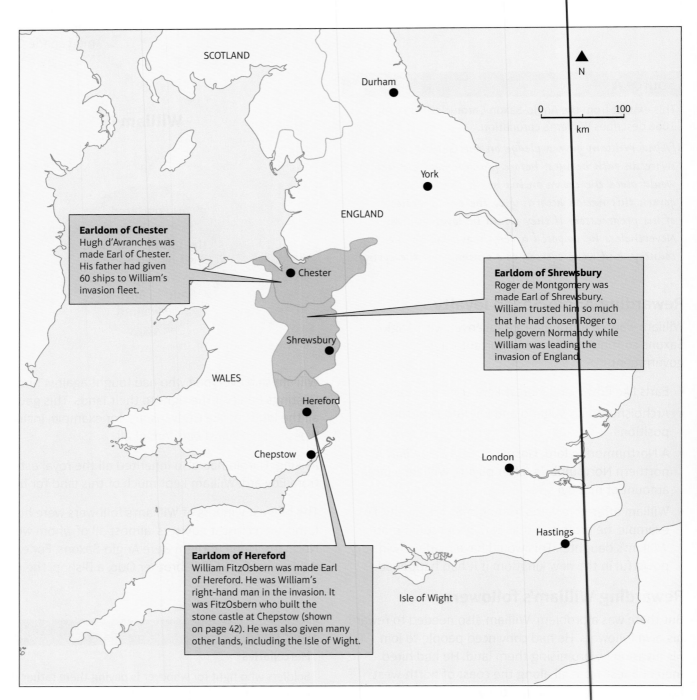

Figure 2.2 The Marcher earldoms of Chester, Shrewsbury and Hereford protected England from Wales.

Earldom of Chester
Hugh d'Avranches was made Earl of Chester. His father had given 60 ships to William's invasion fleet.

Earldom of Shrewsbury
Roger de Montgomery was made Earl of Shrewsbury. William trusted him so much that he had chosen Roger to help govern Normandy while William was leading the invasion of England.

Earldom of Hereford
William FitzOsbern was made Earl of Hereford. He was William's right-hand man in the invasion. It was FitzOsbern who built the stone castle at Chepstow (shown on page 42). He was also given many other lands, including the Isle of Wight.

Key features of the Marcher earldoms

Key feature	Details	Purpose
Shire-sized, centred on shire town	The great earldoms of Anglo-Saxon England were big areas containing several shires. The Marcher earldoms were smaller and more compact.	Their smaller size made them easier to control. This also meant the Marcher earls were not as powerful as the king.
Special privileges to create settlements	The Marcher earldoms gave their earls the rights that usually only the king had. For example: • to create boroughs (towns) and markets • to build churches (replacing Anglo-Saxon ones).	These rights helped the earls to attract people from Normandy to come and live in the borderland regions.
Granted the full power of the law	Usually, sheriffs were the king's officers. But in the Marcher earldoms, sheriffs worked for the earl. Sheriffs controlled the shire courts. This gave the earls almost complete power over the legal system in the earldom.	The earls could respond quickly and firmly to any unrest or disobedience in their earldom.
Exempted from tax	Marcher earls did not have to pay tax to the king on their lands, unlike earls in the rest of England.	To reward their loyalty and encourage the earls to spend money on new settlements and defences.
The right to build castles	In the rest of England, landholders had to ask the king before they could build castles. The Marcher earls were free to build castles wherever they were needed.	Castles were used to control the area and to launch attacks into Wales.

Summary

Why did William create the Marcher earldoms?
• To protect the borderlands (Marches) from the Welsh. Castles were important for this.
• To reward followers – for example, William FitzOsbern was made the Earl of Hereford. The Marcher earls got land, power and money from tax.
• To encourage Normans to move to the borderlands, the Marcher earls could build new towns to attract people from Normandy to the marches.

The Marcher earls had a lot more independence from the king than other earls. That meant they could deal with trouble quickly.

However, they were not the king's equals. They gave their allegiance to the king and had to provide military service for him whenever he asked. They were also not allowed to try people for crimes against the king.

Exam-style question, Section B

Explain why William created the Marcher earldoms.

You may use the following in your answer:

- protecting the borders
- rewarding followers.

You **must** also use information of your own. **12 marks**

Exam tip

This question is about causation (reasons for). Some things in history happened because people intended them to happen. Here you can explain what William wanted to achieve as a result of the creation of the Marcher earldoms. Write an explanation, not a description. Look back at the previous page for help with this.

Reasons for building castles

William used castles to control England. Over 500 castles were built during his reign. Although castles were common in Normandy and north-west Europe, they were almost unknown in Anglo-Saxon England. One of the first things that William did when he invaded was to build a castle at Pevensey, where he landed.

Activities

1. Explain, using the map in Figure 2.3 to help you, why there are many castles near Hereford and Chepstow.

2. Use Figure 2.4 on the opposite page to help you:
   a. plan how you would attack the castle
   b. plan how you would defend it.

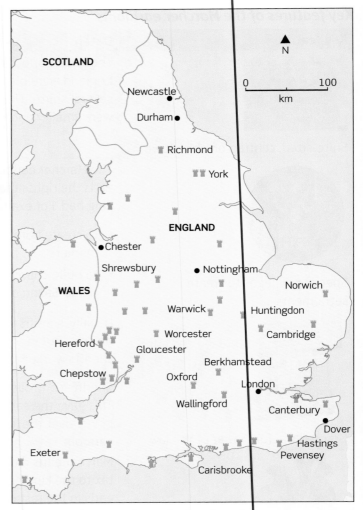

Figure 2.3 This map shows the location of the most important castles built during William's reign.

Key features and advantages of castles

The design of motte* and bailey* castles made them quick to build and difficult to attack.

Key terms

Motte*

The mound of earth that the castle stood on.

Bailey*

The outer part of the castle, surrounding the motte and protected by a fence or wall.

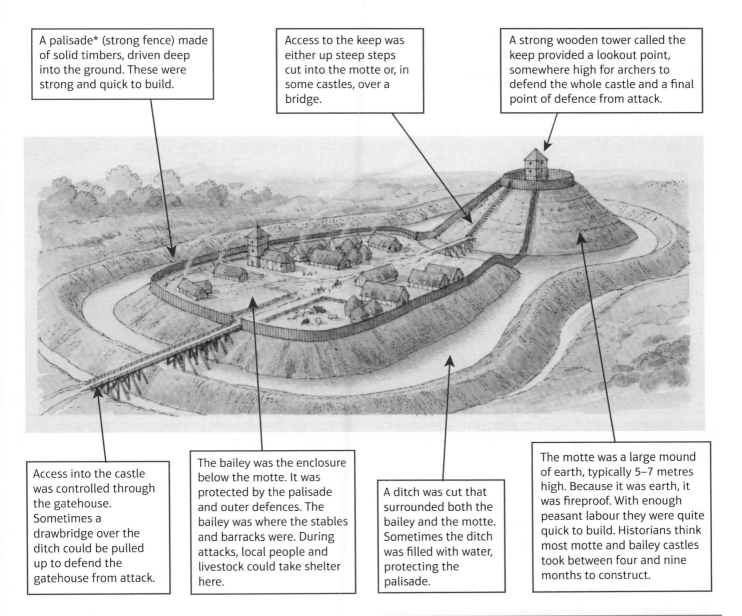

A palisade* (strong fence) made of solid timbers, driven deep into the ground. These were strong and quick to build.

Access to the keep was either up steep steps cut into the motte or, in some castles, over a bridge.

A strong wooden tower called the keep provided a lookout point, somewhere high for archers to defend the whole castle and a final point of defence from attack.

Access into the castle was controlled through the gatehouse. Sometimes a drawbridge over the ditch could be pulled up to defend the gatehouse from attack.

The bailey was the enclosure below the motte. It was protected by the palisade and outer defences. The bailey was where the stables and barracks were. During attacks, local people and livestock could take shelter here.

A ditch was cut that surrounded both the bailey and the motte. Sometimes the ditch was filled with water, protecting the palisade.

The motte was a large mound of earth, typically 5–7 metres high. Because it was earth, it was fireproof. With enough peasant labour they were quite quick to build. Historians think most motte and bailey castles took between four and nine months to construct.

Figure 2.4 Motte and bailey castles were very difficult to attack.

Why were castles important?

- Castles were built in **important locations** – for example, at river crossings or near passes through mountains or hills. The Marcher earls built castles all along the border with Wales, as shown in Figure 2.3.
- Castles were used as a **base** by the lord of the area. The Marcher earls launched invasions into Wales from castles like Chepstow in South Wales. If troops were beaten back, they could take shelter in the castle and then launch a counter-attack.

> ### Key term
>
> **Palisade***
> A high fence made of logs stood on end and hammered into the ground.

- Castles were used to **dominate territory** that Normans wanted to control. These castles were often built in towns, for example Exeter, Warwick, Nottingham and York castles.
- Castles were a **symbol of Norman power**: everyone in the area would see the castle towering over them and would constantly be reminded of who ruled them.

How were castles different from burhs?

Burhs	Castles
Public – maintained by the town to protect everyone.	**Private** – built for the lord and his garrison (his soldiers).
Big – the walls surrounded the whole town.	**Small** – this made them easier to defend.
High fire risk – burhs were hard to get into, but the thatched roofs of the houses inside the walls were easy for attackers to set fire to.	**Lower fire risk** – protected by earth mounds that would not burn. The wooden motte was raised up high – harder to set fire to.
English-protectors – burhs were built to protect all the Anglo-Saxons in their area.	**English-controllers** – castles were built to control all the Anglo-Saxons in their area.

Impacts of castles

- Local people would be forced to build the castle.
- Troops would be based in the castle's garrison, ready to crack down on any troublemakers.
- The local skyline would be dominated by the castle, a constant reminder of who was now in charge.
- When castles were built in towns, houses were knocked down to make room for them.

2.1 Establishing control: summary

- The submission of the earls in 1066 suggested that William could be accepted as king.
- William treated the Anglo-Saxon earls who submitted to him very well, to show that he would reward loyalty.
- William rewarded his Norman followers and supporters too, with land and money.
- William set up new earldoms to help establish control over the English borderlands.
- Castles, new to England, were very important in establishing military control.

Checkpoint

Strengthen

S1 Give three reasons to help explain the submission of the earls.

S2 Give one example of how William rewarded a Norman follower and one example of how he rewarded a loyal Anglo-Saxon.

S3 Describe three features of Norman castles that helped William control England.

Challenge

C1 Explain how the Marcher earldoms were different from Anglo-Saxon earldoms.

How confident do you feel about your answers to these questions? If you are not sure you answered them well, try the following activity.

Activity

The '5Ws' technique is a good way of coming up with ideas, improving your memory and spotting gaps in your knowledge. Ask yourself: who, what, when, where and why? Try doing this for castles.

The revolt of Edwin and Morcar in 1068

In spring 1067, William felt England was secure enough for him to return home to Normandy. He took with him a lot of English treasure.

When William returned to England in December 1067, Norman control was under threat. Herefordshire had been attacked by the Welsh and a rebel Anglo-Saxon thegn called Eadric the Wild.

Events of the revolt

In 1068, Edwin and Morcar fled from William's court. They went north and were joined by many others in rebellion against William. They all protested about the injustice and tyranny of his rule.

We do not know a great deal about the other supporters of this revolt. We know that Earl Waltheof, Earl Gospatric of Northumbria and Edgar Aethling joined Edwin and Morcar in the revolt.

Key term

Castellan*

The governor of a castle and its surrounding lands (castlery).

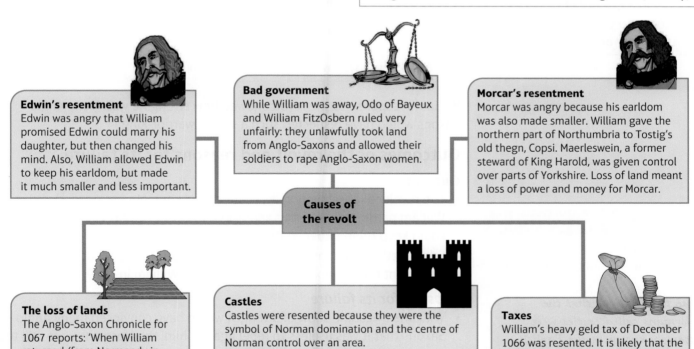

Edwin's resentment
Edwin was angry that William promised Edwin could marry his daughter, but then changed his mind. Also, William allowed Edwin to keep his earldom, but made it much smaller and less important.

Bad government
While William was away, Odo of Bayeux and William FitzOsbern ruled very unfairly: they unlawfully took land from Anglo-Saxons and allowed their soldiers to rape Anglo-Saxon women.

Morcar's resentment
Morcar was angry because his earldom was also made smaller. William gave the northern part of Northumbria to Tostig's old thegn, Copsi. Maerleswein, a former steward of King Harold, was given control over parts of Yorkshire. Loss of land meant a loss of power and money for Morcar.

Causes of the revolt

The loss of lands
The Anglo-Saxon Chronicle for 1067 reports: 'When William returned (from Normandy in 1067) he gave away every man's land'. William's followers grabbed more land, and William allowed this.

Castles
Castles were resented because they were the symbol of Norman domination and the centre of Norman control over an area.
Castleries were set up: units of land controlled by the castellan* of a castle. The castellan could order the people in that area to provide things the castle and its garrison needed. Castle-building in towns also meant knocking down dozens, sometimes hundreds, of homes.

Taxes
William's heavy geld tax of December 1066 was resented. It is likely that the Anglo-Saxon earls who were taken back to Normandy saw that William planned to use English wealth for the good of Normandy. They resented being made poorer so Normandy could get richer.

Figure 2.5 The causes of the revolt of Edwin and Morcar.

Activities ?

1 Imagine you are an Anglo-Saxon thegn in 1068. Create a poster that calls on your fellow Anglo-Saxons to join the rebellion against William and his Normans. Use the information about the causes of the revolt to help you.

2 Look back at the diagram of reasons for the revolt on the previous page.
Sort these reasons into one (or more) of the following categories:
- social and political
- economic (about money, land)
- military.

3 Compare Edwin and Morcar's revolt with Tostig's revolt against Edward and Harold. Come up with at least one similarity and one difference.

What happened next?

1. William was informed of the revolt.

2. William took his forces north, building castles as they went.

3. William went first to Warwick, a key city in Mercia and set about building a castle.

4. Then William went to Nottingham and built another. It was a very successful show of force.

5. Edwin and Morcar were quick to surrender as soon as William had established control of Warwick.

6. The citizens of York sent William hostages to show their obedience as soon as Nottingham had fallen, followed quickly by the Northumbrian rebels.

7. Edgar fled north to Scotland, where Malcolm III took him in; the others begged William for forgiveness.

8. The revolt was over, but resistance continued.

William's response to the revolt showed how strong he was. Many Anglo-Saxons would have respected such a strong warrior-king.

Outcomes of the revolt and reasons for its failure

Outcomes
- The revolt collapsed very quickly after Edwin and Morcar surrendered. William pardoned them, but kept them as 'guests' at his court, where he could keep them under control.
- Edgar Aethling and other rebel leaders escaped to Scotland. This was important for the next big rebellion against William in 1069.

Reasons for its failure
- William's awesome show of strength would have convinced many Anglo-Saxons that it was useless to rebel against him: the Normans were still too strong.
- Why did Edwin and Morcar surrender so quickly? Maybe their revolt of 1068 was a test to see whether William was able to respond. When William reacted so quickly and strongly, the revolt was called off.
- We know that although Anglo-Saxons were excellent warriors, they had no idea how to attack castles (see Source A).

Source A

An Anglo-Norman English chronicler, Orderic Vitalis, writing soon after the revolt.

The fortifications that the Normans called castles were scarcely known in the English provinces, and so the English – in spite of their courage and love of fighting – could put up only a weak resistance to their enemies.

Edgar the Aethling and the rebellions in the North, 1069

In the spring of 1069, rebellions began in the North that were extremely dangerous for William.

- There were rebellions in Northumbria.
- Edgar the Aethling came down from Scotland. His troops and the rebels from Northumbria joined forces.
- King Sweyn of Denmark sent a fleet of ships and warriors led by his brother, Asbjorn. This enormous force teamed up with Edgar and the other rebels.

The death of Robert Cumin

William chose a new earl of Northern Northumbria in 1068: Robert Cumin, one of his supporters.

- In January 1069, Cumin took a large force north, attacking towns and villages on his way.
- When he got to Durham, the bishop warned him his violence had made the people angry, but Cumin ignored him. This was a serious mistake.
- A band of Northumbrians made a surprise attack on the Normans in the streets of Durham.
- Cumin took shelter in the bishop's house, but the rebels set fire to it and killed him.

The uprising in York

Soon after a similar uprising happened in York, which killed the governor and many Norman troops.

- Edgar the Aethling and his supporters came down from Scotland and joined the rebels.
- They attacked the Norman sheriff and his garrison. William then arrived very quickly with a large army.
- William easily defeated the rebels, with the whole city of York being 'laid to waste'.
- Edgar escaped back to Scotland.
- A new castle was rapidly built in York, with William FitzOsbern as its castellan.

The king decided that FitzOsbern would be able to keep the North under control while he returned to Winchester to celebrate Easter. But he had underestimated the threat to his rule. The Northern rebellions were far from over.

Timeline

The rebellions in the North, 1069

31 January Earl Cumin is killed in Durham

c February Uprising in York. Edgar joins uprising from Scotland. William defeats York rebels

13 April William back in Winchester for Easter

c 8 September Danish fleet invades on the east coast

21 September Combined Anglo–Danish army arrives at York

c December William pays the Danes to go away

Events of the rebellions

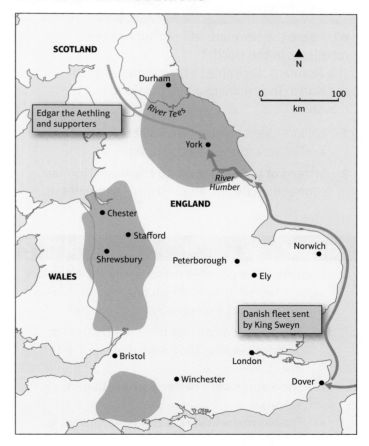

Figure 2.6 The rebellions started in the North, but also included Shropshire in the west, the south-west and Staffordshire in the north Midlands (marked in purple).

The Anglo–Danish attack on York

1. Through the summer of 1069, King Sweyn of Denmark assembled a fleet, which arrived on the English coast at the start of September.

2. The Danes met up with Edgar the Aethling's troops (down again from Scotland) in mid-September. This co-ordinated attack was a significant threat to William.

3. The combined army marched on York, reaching it on 21 September. The Norman defenders accidentally set fire to the city. Perhaps because their defences were damaged in the fire, the Normans went out to meet the Anglo–Danish army and were cut to pieces. An estimated 3,000 Normans were killed and both castles were destroyed. William's control of England was under enormous pressure.

4. After victory in York, the Danes sailed across the Humber to the coast of Lincolnshire. This was a very swampy area which was difficult to get to by land. The Danes waited there to see what would happen next. The Anglo-Saxon rebels scattered. As William's army hunted them down, news came in of a series of other rebellions in Devon and the earldoms of Shrewsbury and Chester (see Figure 2.6).

5. But as soon as William and his troops arrived in a rebel area, the rebels disappeared. Once William left for another rebel hotspot, the rebellion started again. Meanwhile, William could not attack the Danes by land (because of swamps, see next page), and attacking Vikings at sea would be foolish – the Danes were brilliant sailors, and the Normans were not.

Summary

Why were the Normans able to survive the rebellions in the North?

The Normans were able to hold onto control of the North. They managed this thanks to two main reasons:

1 William's leadership: when William led troops into a rebel area, the rebels scattered.

2 Instead of pressing south to challenge Norman control directly, the Anglo-Danish army split up.

Activities ?

1 Here are three possible reasons why the Normans were defeated at York. Which one do you think is the best reason? Explain why.
   - The Normans couldn't use their castles for defence because they were damaged in the fire.
   - The Vikings were better warriors than Anglo-Saxons.
   - The Normans in York didn't have William to lead them.

2 Explain who you think was the bigger threat to William: the Anglo-Saxons or the Danes.

William's solution

William was more worried about the Danes than the Anglo-Saxons. He had beaten Anglo-Saxons in battle many times. But the North was half-Danish. That meant the North might support a Danish invasion, and work with the Danes against the Normans. To solve the problem, William did the following:

- He paid the Danes a large amount of money to leave.
- He started a campaign of total destruction known as the 'Harrying* of the North' in the winter of 1069–70.

During the Harrying, crops were burnt in the fields, destroying seed crops and killing livestock.

- William wanted to make life impossible in the North.
- This meant if the Danes came back, there would be no supplies and nobody to help them.

Thousands of people died of starvation as a result. Other consequences of the Harrying of the North are on page 59.

Key term

Harrying*

An old word meaning to 'lay waste' to something, to devastate it.

Hereward the Wake and rebellion at Ely, 1070–71

The return of the Danes

In 1070, a Danish fleet returned to England, this time with King Sweyn himself as its leader. Instead of heading to Northumbria, Sweyn set up on the Isle of Ely, in the middle of the Fens in East Anglia. This was a good defensive location because:

- Ely was surrounded by water and swamps
- only locals knew the safe paths through the swamps to get to Ely.

Hereward the Wake

East Anglia was part of the Danelaw and Sweyn made alliances with the local people, including a rebel leader called Hereward the Wake.

- Hereward was a local thegn who had been exiled before the Norman invasion. When he returned to England in 1069 he found that his lands had been seized and given to a Norman.
- Using the Fenland swamps to help him, Hereward had been fighting a guerrilla war* against the Normans with other East Anglia rebels.

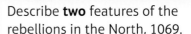

Exam-style question, Section B

Describe **two** features of the rebellions in the North, 1069.

4 marks

Exam tip

This question is about key features and characteristics. Remember to give supporting information for each feature. For example: the main rebellion combined Anglo-Saxon and Danish forces, led by Edgar Aethling and Asbjorn of Denmark.

Key term

Guerrilla war*

When small groups attack a larger force by surprise and then disappear back into the local population. It is a modern term.

Source B

This photo shows Ely cathedral today when the river is flooded; you can see that Ely is on higher ground surrounded by swampy wetland. The Normans started building Ely cathedral in 1083.

Threats and responses

The rebellion at Ely in 1070–71 meant new threats for William and Norman control of England. William dealt with each threat in a different way. The outcomes were a big success for William.

Threat 1: the Danish invasion

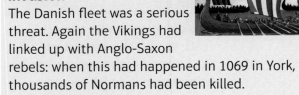

The Danish fleet was a serious threat. Again the Vikings had linked up with Anglo-Saxon rebels: when this had happened in 1069 in York, thousands of Normans had been killed.

What did William do?

He paid the Danes to go away. This approach had worked in the short-term in 1069.

What was the outcome?

The Anglo-Saxon rebels were easier to defeat once the Danes had left – they didn't have Viking support.

Threat 2: 'guerrilla warfare' from the Anglo-Saxon rebels

The Anglo-Saxon rebels avoided getting into a battle with the Normans. Instead they used what we would call guerrilla tactics, for example attacking when Norman patrols were tired, and then hiding out in local villages.

When William and his troops turned up, the rebel attacks stopped. When he went away to another trouble spot, the rebel attacks began again.

What did William do?

- 'Harrying' the local area meant no more local villages for rebels to hide in.
- Troops searched out rebel hideouts.
- Castles were built which meant Norman patrols had a safe base.
- William used trusted followers to put down the unrest in one area, while he and his troops went off to deal with more serious trouble somewhere else.

What was the outcome?

William decided that local Anglo-Saxon lords and thegns could not be trusted. He replaced them with Normans.

Threat 3: discontent from troops and followers

William's troops complained about marching all over the countryside, chasing after the rebels. They complained even more in winter. There was a risk that some might stop supporting William – especially mercenaries who William was paying to fight for him.

What did William do?

- He promised them land and other rewards.
- His leadership skills motivated his troops.
- Building castles gave the troops safe places to stay along their marches.

What was the outcome?

- More land was taken from Anglo-Saxons to reward William's followers.
- Money to pay William's troops came from more taxes and also wealth taken from Anglo-Saxon churches.

Threat 4: Edgar the Aethling as the 'real' king

William really wanted to be accepted as England's proper king. Edgar the Aethling was a threat because he had been crowned king of England (see page 43). Now Edgar was encouraging rebellions against William.

What did William do?

- He did lots of royal things, so people would see him being king. For example, he led the celebrations for Easter at Winchester in 1069, which is something Anglo-Saxon kings had done before.
- It must have been very important for William to lead the Easter celebrations. We know this because he left York in 1069, as soon as the rebellion had been defeated, to travel down to Winchester.

What was the outcome?

- Many English people followed William against the rebels. Some Anglo-Saxon thegns defended their towns against the rebels.
- We also know that William built up his armies using Anglo-Saxon recruits.
- This suggests many English people did come to accept William as having the right to be king.

The attack on Peterborough and fall of Ely

The Danes and Hereward raided Peterborough Abbey. Hereward wanted to stop its riches falling into the hands of the Normans.

The end of the Anglo-Saxon rebellions

The defeat of the rebels at Ely marked the end of the Anglo-Saxon rebellions. Eadric the Wild (see page 51) also abandoned his rebellion against the Marcher earls, possibly after being beaten in battle.

William defeats the rebels

- The Danes sailed with all the treasure back to Denmark.
- Hereward was joined by Morcar and his men.
- As the Normans advanced, led by William, Hereward and Morcar prepared to defend the Isle of Ely.
- The Normans managed to capture Ely, possibly by bribing local monks to show them a safe way through the marshes.
- Ely was captured, along with Morcar. Hereward escaped, and was not heard of again.

2.2 The causes and outcomes of Anglo-Saxon resistance: summary

- The years 1068–71 involved rebellion due mainly to resentment over land.
- Edwin and Morcar's revolt in 1068 collapsed quickly.
- The Northern rebellions of 1069 and Ely in 1070–71 were very serious because of the involvement of Danish invasion fleets.
- William's brutal tactics were successful in ending the Anglo-Saxon rebellions.

Checkpoint

Strengthen

S1 Identify two causes of Anglo-Saxon resistance in the period 1068–71.

S2 How do you think William's attitude to Earl Edwin changed from 1066 to 1071? Draw a graph, with time along the bottom axis from 1066 to 1071 and William's feelings on the vertical axis, ranging from very positive at the top to very negative at the bottom.

S3 Describe two ways in which William successfully dealt with Anglo-Saxon rebellions.

Challenge

C1 Explain why the Anglo-Saxon earls and Edgar were not able to win against William.

How confident do you feel about your answers to these questions? If you are not sure you answered them well, try the activity below.

Activity ?

Many similar events happened in a short period of time in 1068–71. Create your own timeline for the period to help get the events straight and identify the links between each event.

The Harrying of the North, 1069–70

Reasons for the Harrying of the North

Punishment for rebelling against William.

As a warning to other areas of England not to rebel against Norman control.

Revenge for the murder of Robert Cumin and thousands of other Normans at York.

Five reasons for the Harrying of the North

To stop the Danes using Northumbria as a base for attacks in the future.

To tackle Anglo-Saxon 'guerrilla' tactics, by leaving them no bases in the North.

William is reported to have regretted his decision to 'lay waste' to the North for the rest of his life. He may have been acting out of anger and frustration rather than carrying out a careful plan.

Although these were violent times, the Harrying shocked people at the time. It was so brutal. People who had nothing to do with the rebellion suffered terribly.

The Harrying of the North created a disaster zone for many years after.

Source A

When the Normans landed on the south coast, they burned down houses in Wessex, as shown in this scene from the Bayeux Tapestry. The Harrying of the North was similar, but on a much bigger scale.

Short-term impacts of the Harrying

The short-term impacts of the Harrying of the North were like a natural disaster. It is thought that as many as 100,000 people died.

> ### Short-term impacts of the Harrying
> - People starved to death because the Normans burned their crops and killed their livestock.
> - People also died because the Normans had burned down their houses and they had nowhere to shelter.
> - William's troops destroyed seeds. That meant there was no hope of starting again by planting new crops. Thousands of refugees fled the region.
> - There were reports of cannibalism and of people selling themselves into slavery for food.

Source B

Chronicler Symeon of Durham recorded the events.

It was horrible to observe, in houses, streets and roads, human corpses rotting... For no-one survived to cover them with earth, all having perished by the sword and starvation, or left the land of their fathers because of hunger.

Long-term impacts of the Harrying of the North, 1069–87

> ### Long-term impacts of the Harrying
> - There were no more uprisings in Northumbria.
> - Almost 20 years later, the area still had not recovered. The Domesday survey showed 60% of Northumbria was not being farmed in 1086.
> - There were between 80,000 and 150,000 fewer people in 1086 than in January 1066.
> - There were no more Danish invasions of Northumbria.
> - William never trusted Anglo-Saxon aristocrats again and began replacing them with loyal Normans.
> - The Harrying of the North was widely criticised, including by the pope. William spent a lot of time trying to show he was sorry for the Harrying. For example, he gave a lot of money to the Church.

Activity

How would a modern-day news report cover the Harrying of the North? Write a script for a report involving the following:

- a news anchor role to introduce the story and set it in context
- a reporter role, giving an eye-witness account of events
- short interviews with a Northern refugee and a Norman soldier
- a statement from William's government.

Exam-style question, Section B

'The main reason for the Harrying of the North was to prevent another Danish invasion'.

How far do you agree? Explain your answer.

You may use the following in your answer:

- Robert Cumin
- Danelaw.

You **must** also use information of your own. **16 marks**

Exam tip

This is a question about causation. Include your own information, as well as arguments prompted by the bullet points. Here are some possible sentence starters you could use in your answer:

- Another reason for the Harrying was revenge for the death of Robert Cumin...
- Another reason was because William wanted to stop rebellions elsewhere...
- In my opinion, the main reason was... because...

Changes in landownership from Anglo-Saxon to Norman, 1066–87

A landholding revolution

Between 1066 and 1087, the Normans replaced the Anglo-Saxons as landholders. By 1087:

- over half of all the land in England was held by about 190 tenants-in-chief*. Only two of them were Anglo-Saxons (Thurkill of Arden and Colswein of Lincoln)

- a quarter of the land was held by the Church. Normans held most senior Church positions
- the king's royal estates made up one-fifth of the land
- less than 5% of the land was still held by Anglo-Saxon aristocrats, typically in small estates.

Key term

Tenants-in-chief*

The large landholders of Norman England who held their land directly from the king.

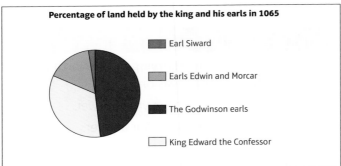

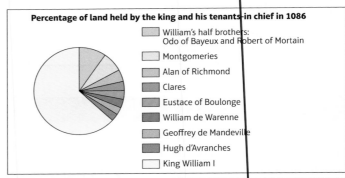

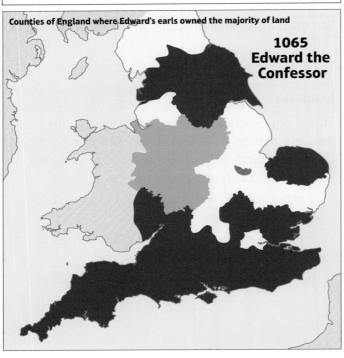

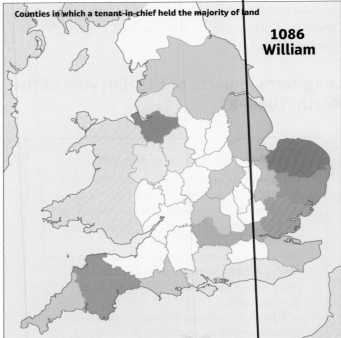

Figure 2.7 The change in landownership between 1066 and 1086.

Landownership and rebellion

The rebellions of 1068, 1069 and 1070–71 showed William that the Anglo-Saxon earls could not be trusted. He took their lands and gave them to his followers. Without land, the Anglo-Saxon aristocrats had no money, no thegns, no power.

Before 1066, there were around 4,000 thegns in England.

- The rebellions showed that, if earls rebelled, so did their thegns.
- Hereward the Wake and Eadric the Wild were powerful thegns who led rebellions of their own.
- By 1087, these 4,000 thegns were no longer a threat. Their Anglo-Saxon lords had almost all been replaced by Normans. Most thegns now only had a small amount of land. They had to obey their Norman lords if they wanted to keep that land.

How did Anglo-Saxons lose their land?

Anglo-Saxons lost their land to Normans in three main ways. Two of these ways were legal, which was important to William's claims to being a just and fair king.

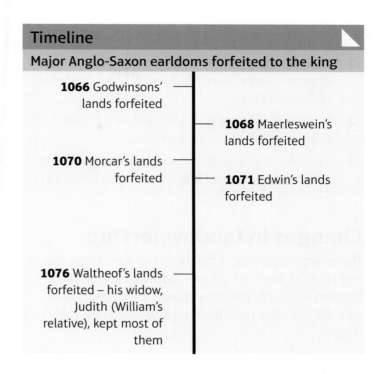

Timeline

Major Anglo-Saxon earldoms forfeited to the king

1066 Godwinsons' lands forfeited

1068 Maerleswein's lands forfeited

1070 Morcar's lands forfeited

1071 Edwin's lands forfeited

1076 Waltheof's lands forfeited – his widow, Judith (William's relative), kept most of them

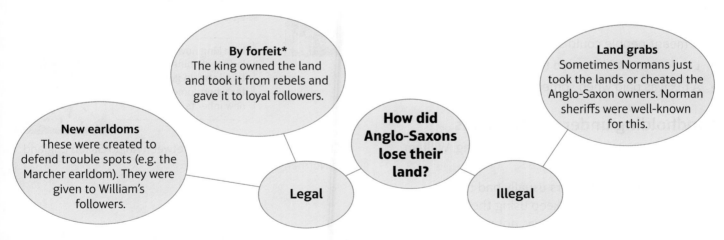

New earldoms
These were created to defend trouble spots (e.g. the Marcher earldom). They were given to William's followers.

By forfeit*
The king owned the land and took it from rebels and gave it to loyal followers.

Land grabs
Sometimes Normans just took the lands or cheated the Anglo-Saxon owners. Norman sheriffs were well-known for this.

How did Anglo-Saxons lose their land?

Legal

Illegal

Changes in landholding after 1071

After the Battle of Hastings, William had been able to put Normans in control of Godwinson lands in the South and West. After the rebellions of 1068 to 1071, William could hand out forfeited lands throughout Mercia, East Anglia and the North.

William also changed the way he granted out the land to increase Norman control.

- He put the forfeited land into blocks of territory rather than it being scattered around the country.

- These blocks were much better for imposing control because there was a single strong authority over the whole area.

After 1071, William used landownership to increase Norman control.

Key term

Forfeit*

To lose something as a punishment for committing a crime or bad action.

Activities ?

1 Link these together in a sentence that explains a change in landownership: Godwinsons + forfeit + tenants-in-chief.

2 Two old thegns meet in 1072. Role-play their conversation about the Normans.

3 Explain why changing who controlled the land reduced the chance of Anglo-Saxon revolt after 1071.

Changes in landownership

There were important differences between Anglo-Saxon and Norman England in how landownership worked. Norman landlords got more power. Any Anglo-Saxon who did not obey their Norman lord could lose their land.

Anglo-Saxon landholding

In Edward the Confessor's time, people could own their land. The Church could also own its land.

- This meant land could be passed on (inherited): when a thegn died, his son could inherit the land.
- It meant people could sell their land.
- Landowners still needed to pay geld tax on their land.
- A tax was paid when someone inherited the land.

Landholding under the Normans

- There was only one landowner – the king. William owned all the land.
- Anglo-Saxon landholders usually had to pay William for the right to keep using their land (called redeeming the land). This was not popular!
- When William granted land to his followers, they did not have to redeem it. However, their heir had to pay a tax to the king.

William was very powerful under this new system. William enforced the laws much more strictly. If people did not do as the king wished, they could lose their lands and be left with nothing.

Anglo-Saxon England

This writ is a document that proves my right to this land. When I die, I'll pass it on to my son. He'll have the right to this land, then.

This writ proves my church owns this field. That means we can sell the field if we want to.

Norman England

Apparently, I have to pay King William for my land now! If I want to use my own land, I have to redeem it first. This is outrageous!

I'm a Norman – I fought with William to make him king. So why should my eldest son have to pay William a tax to keep using MY land?

I am king now. Since the land is all mine, it's right that I should get paid a tax when someone new inherits land.

► Changes in land ownership between Anglo-Saxon England and Norman England.

Money...	Money...	Return land	Return land
to redeem land	to inherit land	dying without an heir	forfeiture

WILLIAM

Figure 2.8 Changes to the land holding system reinforced William's control as king.

Landholding under the tenants-in-chief

It wasn't only the king who had this power. His tenants-in-chief had a lot of power, too. When they took over new lands, all the thegns there had a new lord.

- When a thegn died, their tenant-in-chief was allowed to choose who got their land next. Tenants-in-chief made their followers 'heirs' to the thegn's land.
- They could take land away from thegns who did not do what the tenant-in-chief ordered.

Thegns might cling on to some land but their way of life was completely changed. Many left England to work as mercenaries in Europe. Those that stayed had to be obedient vassals* to their new lords if they wanted to survive.

Key term

Vassal*
Someone who held their land in return for services to their Norman lord.

Summary

- Changing landownership made Anglo-Saxon thegns poorer and more dependent on their new lords.
- The changes made William very powerful and increased Norman control.

Changes for the peasants

How did life change for peasants under the Normans?

Anglo-Saxon England	Norman England
Most peasants farm land for their lords in return for land to farm for themselves.	Most peasants still farm land for their Norman lords in return for land to farm for themselves, but the Normans make more demands on them.
Some peasants could afford to rent land from their lord and became independent farmers.	It became rarer and rarer for peasants to stay independent. Norman lords made the peasants work for them. They did not allow them to stay independent.

Source B

This picture of ploughing is from an 11th-century calendar, which was probably created in Winchester. Under the Normans, most peasants came to depend on their lord instead of paying rent and farming their land independently.

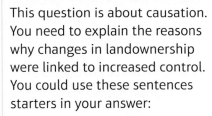

Exam-style question, Section B

Explain why changes in landownership made resistance to Norman control less likely after 1071.

You may use the following in your answer:

- tenants-in-chief
- thegns.

You **must** also use information of your own. **12 marks**

Exam tip

This question is about causation. You need to explain the reasons why changes in landownership were linked to increased control. You could use these sentences starters in your answer:

- Tenants-in-chief made resistance to Norman control less likely because if thegns didn't obey their tenant-in-chief then…
- Many thegns left England because of changes to landownership. This made resistance less likely because it meant any rebellious thegns…
- The king owned all the land in England. This made resistance to Norman control less likely because…

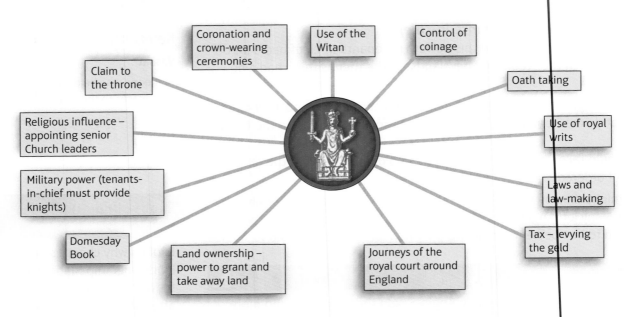

Figure 2.9 The powers of King William I. The image in the middle is a representation of William's royal seal.

Maintaining royal power

Military strength

William used his military skill and his ruthlessness to crush rebellions.

- Anglo-Saxons had huge respect for great warriors
- William's skill and luck in battle would have proved to many in England that God was on his side.
- William's military power explains why many Anglo-Saxons joined his armies against the rebels.

The legitimate successor

William wanted people to accept him as king. He said God had chosen him.

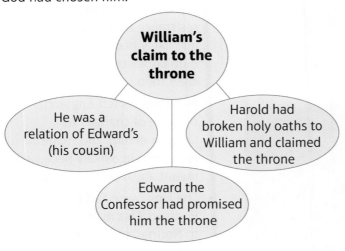

▶ William as the legitimate successor.

Activity ?

Congratulations: you have invaded another country and been crowned by its archbishop. What actions will you now take to promote yourself as king?

Royal ceremonies

At his coronation, William was anointed† with sacred oil. This was to show that he was king by the will of God.

William started a new custom of being seen in public wearing his crown three times a year. These were at the most important times of the Christian calendar (over Easter and Christmas) and in important places (Winchester, Westminster, Gloucester).

Key term

Anointed*

Part of a religious ceremony where a person has holy oil put on them.

Coinage and writs

William took control of the minting of coins – minting is the word for making coins.

- The coins had an image of William on them, as did his royal seal.
- The seal was attached to the king's writs (official documents and proclamations).
- The seal showed William on his throne on one side and as a knight, mounted on a horse, on the other

Normandy did not have a system like writs, but in England William clearly found them a good way of spreading his royal power across the whole country.

Journeys around England

The king and royal court travelled around the country, meeting with important local families and officials. The arrival of the king in a region was a very big occasion. People from each region would see William being their king.

Owning the land

William was the owner of all the land in England. Now everyone who held land was connected to the king.

This connection was much stronger than in Edward the Confessor's time. William took back land from rebels or those who had died without heirs, granting it out again to followers. He also was the only judge of any complaints about how his land was being used.

Oath-taking

Oaths were taken very seriously and William held oath-taking ceremonies in which all men would swear to serve him loyally.

- The biggest was in 1086, when William was worried about another great Viking invasion.
- The ceremony was held at Salisbury and every landholder came and swore their loyalty to the king.
- This must have involved hundreds of men, possibly thousands.

2.3 The legacy of resistance: summary

- Anglo-Saxon resistance convinced William that sharing power would not work.
- The Harrying of the North showed how ruthless William could be.
- Changing landownership made thegns poorer and more dependent on their new lords.
- Military skill and strength was behind William's royal power.

Checkpoint

Strengthen

S1 Describe one immediate impact of the Harrying of the North and one long-term impact.

S2 Imagine you are a tenant-in-chief hoping to convince more Normans to come over to live on your new estates in England. Create a poster explaining the advantages.

S3 Compare the information about William's royal power here with the information about Anglo-Saxon kings on pages 11–12. What are the similarities and differences?

Challenge

C1 Explain how changes in landownership made Anglo-Saxon rebellions less likely to occur.

Activity

When we read information from a book, website or our notes, it is tempting to think 'yes, I know all this' or 'I get what this is about'. A great way to **really** find out what you do remember and how much you actually understand is to try and tell someone else about it. Try explaining how William kept control of England to a partner. If there are any gaps in what you can explain, go back to your notes and fill those gaps.

2.4 Revolt of the Earls, 1075

Learning outcomes

- Understand the reasons for and features of the Revolt of the Earls, 1075.
- Understand why the revolt was defeated and the effects of the revolt.

The conspirators

The revolt of 1075 was very different from the rebellions of 1068–71. In the revolt of 1075, Normans rebelled against William and many Anglo-Saxons defended their king. For that reason, the revolt of 1075 is sometimes known as 'the revolt of the Norman Earls'.

- The rebellion's leader was Ralph de Gael, Earl of East Anglia.
- Ralph plotted with Roger de Breteuil, Earl of Hereford, and Waltheof, Earl of Northumbria, to overthrow William and divide the kingdom into three between them.
- Ralph also asked the Danes for help, who put together an impressive invasion fleet.
- The rebels also had support from Normandy's rivals, Brittany and France. Both states wanted to weaken Normandy.

Ralph de Gael, Earl of East Anglia

Ralph's father was rewarded with lands in East Anglia by William in 1066. Ralph's mother was from Brittany and Ralph was brought up there.

- When his father died, Ralph became Earl of East Anglia, in around 1069.
- In 1075, Ralph married the sister of Roger de Breteuil.

NORMAN

Roger de Breteuil, Earl of Hereford

Roger was the son of William FitzOsbern.

- FitzOsbern was one of William's most loyal and trusted followers.
- William made him Earl of Hereford, a Marcher earldom with huge powers.
- FitzOsbern died in 1071, and Roger became Earl of Hereford.

NORMAN

Waltheof, Earl of Northumbria

Waltheof was the son of Earl Siward.

- Waltheof submitted to William in 1066 and he was allowed to stay as Earl of Northamptonshire.
- In 1069, he was part of the rebellions in the North, but he submitted again to William and was pardoned.
- In 1072, William made Waltheof Earl of Northumbria – perhaps as a gesture of reconciliation* after the Harrying of the North.

SAXON

Key term

Reconciliation*
To find ways for former enemies to forgive each other.

Reasons for the revolt

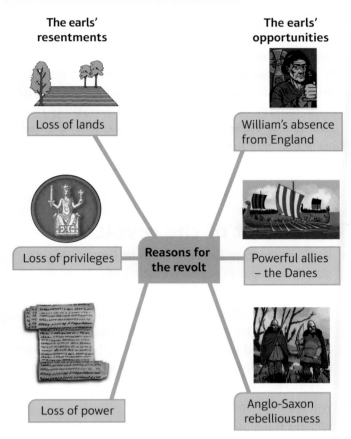

The earls' resentments

Loss of lands

Loss of privileges

Loss of power

Reasons for the revolt

The earls' opportunities

William's absence from England

Powerful allies – the Danes

Anglo-Saxon rebelliousness

Figure 2.10 The reasons for the revolt were connected to the earls' resentments and opportunities.

Roger's motives

- Roger was angry that he got less land for his earldom than William had granted to his father.
- William had tried to reduce the power of Roger's family now that FitzOsbern was dead.
- William had introduced his own sheriffs into the Marcher earldoms, where before the earls had controlled everything for themselves.
- This explains why the plan of the rebels in 1075 was to split the country into three great estates – one each.

Ralph's motives

Ralph's motives are not well known. We can assume that he also resented losing power and wealth compared to his father's holdings.

- He might also have sided with Brittany, where he grew up, against Normandy.

Waltheof's motives

Waltheof seems to have played both sides.

- At first he may have used his contacts in Denmark and with Anglo-Saxon aristocrats to support the revolt.
- He then chose to inform on the revolt to William. This may have been because he thought the revolt was not going to succeed.

Exam-style question, Section B

Describe **two** features of the Revolt of the Earls in 1075. **4 marks**

Exam tip

This question is about identifying key features. Your answer should identify each feature and give some supporting information about it. Here are some features you could use in your answer – details need to be added:

- Unlike earlier revolts, the Revolt of the Earls saw Normans rebelling against William.
- Both Ralph de Gael and Roger de Breteuil resented losing land.
- The revolt involved the Norman earls forming alliances with others.

The events of the revolt

Ralph's wedding feast

Ralph married Emma, the sister of Roger de Breteuil, in 1075. There was a very big wedding feast. Important bishops, abbots, earls and magnates* were invited, including Earl Waltheof.

During the wedding feast, Ralph and Roger told Waltheof of their plans to start a revolt against William. Between the three of them, their lands stretched from west to east and from the far north to the Midlands.

Key term

Magnate*

The historical term for a great man, an important and influential figure.

Ralph and Roger expected that Anglo-Saxons would support their revolt. Waltheof probably had the job of organising the Anglo-Saxons and encouraging the Danes to attack. He was the last surviving Anglo-Saxon earl, with strong contacts with King Sweyn in Denmark, too.

The rebels timed their revolt for when William was in Normandy, leaving Archbishop Lanfranc in charge of England as William's regent.

The plan unfolds

Unfortunately for the earls, their revolt did not get much Anglo-Saxon support. Also the Danish fleet arrived too late. The revolt was defeated before it really began:

- Waltheof told Archbishop Lanfranc about the plot.
- Lanfranc's men checked in Hereford and East Anglia. They saw troops getting ready and castle defences being strengthened.
- Lanfranc wrote letters to Roger. He tried to convince Roger not to rebel against William.
- In the West, Bishop Wulfstan of Worcester and the abbot of Evesham used their troops to prevent Roger crossing the River Severn. That meant Roger and his troops could not leave Herefordshire.
- In the East, Normans and Anglo-Saxons joined together to stop Ralph from breaking out of East Anglia. The Anglo-Saxon Chronicle for 1075 describes the situation for Ralph in Source A.
- William then returned to England. At about this time, the Danes arrived – a huge fleet of 200 ships. But they were too late to help the revolt.
- The Danish leaders did not dare to fight against William.
- Rather than invade, the fleet raided along the east coast, as usual, and sacked York cathedral before going home again.

Source A

The Worcester version of the Anglo-Saxon Chronicle for the year 1075 (adapted).

Ralph tried to move his troops from East Anglia out for battle, but the garrisons of the Norman castles which were in England, together with the inhabitants of the country, opposed them and did everything they could to stop them, so that nothing was accomplished and Ralph only just managed to escape to his ships at Norwich.

The defeat of the revolt

- Ralph escaped to Brittany. His wife, Emma (Roger's sister), held out in Norwich castle until she could make a deal for a safe journey to Brittany.
- Waltheof fled abroad. William tricked him into thinking that he would be forgiven if he came back and submitted to the king. When Waltheof did come back, he was imprisoned. Then he was executed in May 1076.
- William imprisoned Roger for life.
- William travelled back to Normandy and attacked Ralph's castle. But the castle was too strong and William had to retreat. Military victory proved far harder for William to achieve back home than in England.

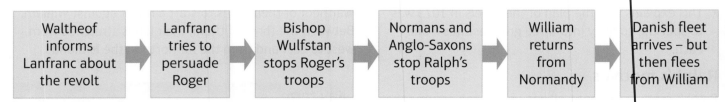

| Waltheof informs Lanfranc about the revolt | → | Lanfranc tries to persuade Roger | → | Bishop Wulfstan stops Roger's troops | → | Normans and Anglo-Saxons stop Ralph's troops | → | William returns from Normandy | → | Danish fleet arrives – but then flees from William |

▶ The defeat of the revolt.

Activities ?

1 Create a storyboard for a short film about the events and defeat of the Revolt of the Earls.

2 In groups, role-play the plotting at Ralph's wedding feast between the three earls. Each earl should give a speech about their own complaints against William.

3 Do you think William was right to execute Waltheof? Explain your answer – try to use a fact or facts to back up your view.

THINKING HISTORICALLY Cause and Consequence (4a&b)

Work on your own and answer the questions below. When you have answered the questions, discuss the answers in a group. Then have a class vote.

1 Read about the killing of Robert Cumin and the start of rebellions in the North in 1061 (page 53).

   a Why was the killing important as a cause of the rebellions?

   b If the killing of Robert Cumin had not happened, would the rebellions in the North still have happened?

2 Look at the information on page 54. The Normans were forced to fight against the Anglo-Saxons and Danes because York castle was damaged. The Normans were defeated.

   a How important was the fire that damaged the castle in explaining the defeat of the Normans?

   b What might have happened if the castle's defences had not been damaged?

3 Look at these other reasons for the rebellions in the North in 1069. How might the rebellions in the North have developed differently if these factors had not been present?

   • William choosing a Norman as the new earl of Northumbria.

   • Edgar the Aethling coming to Northumbria to join the rebellion.

   • William leaving York to celebrate Easter at Winchester.

The effects of the revolt

The Revolt of the Earls suggests some significant changes had happened in Norman England:

- William now needed to be careful of his own earls. Roger and Ralph's revolt was because they resented William keeping power to himself. From this point on, rebellion against William and his sons came from the Norman magnates.
- Anglo-Saxons joined the loyal Normans in stopping the revolts from spreading. The involvement of Anglo-Saxon men like Bishop Wulfstan also suggests that some Anglo-Saxons now supported the Normans.

- The failure of the planned Danish invasion in 1075 was, in fact, the end of the Viking threat to England. But William did not know this. William saw the events of 1075 as very threatening. He kept a tight grip on England.

Threats to me, by William I
1. Normans who want more power. Probably the biggest threat – just like in Normandy…
2. Vikings – although the Danes are scared of fighting me!
3. Anglo-Saxons – maybe not much of a threat now? V. pleased so many English were loyal to me in 1075.

2.4 The legacy of resistance: summary

- The Revolt of the Earls in 1075 was linked to William's policy of reducing the size of earldoms and the power of earls. He wanted to be much stronger than his earls.
- The revolt was extremely threatening for William. It linked three powerful earls, a large invasion force of Danes, and support from Brittany and France.
- Anglo-Saxons supported William and William's reputation (and the failure of the earls' revolt) stopped the Danes from doing more than raiding the eastern coast.

Checkpoint

Strengthen

S1 Who were the earls who led the Revolt of the Earls and where were they earls of?

S2 William had originally given Marcher earls like William FitzOsbern much greater powers than other earls. Name three of these greater powers.

S3 Identify three reasons for the Revolt of the Earls and three reasons for its defeat.

Challenge

C1 Why do you think William had Waltheof executed? What had changed from Waltheof's previous rebellions?

How confident do you feel about your answers to these questions? If you are not sure you answered them well, try the following activity.

Activity

Point, Evidence, Explain (PEE): use this when you are making your notes, as well as when you are writing something for assessment, because it gets you thinking in the right way. For example: resentment at loss of power and wealth was an important reason for the Revolt of the Earls in 1075. What evidence could you use to back that point up? How could you then explain why it is an important reason? Apply this method to your notes from this section.

Recall quiz

1 Who did the Witan first name as king after Harold's death?

2 Where did William receive the submission of the earls?

3 Name the three Marcher earldoms.

4 Name three features of a motte and bailey castle that made them difficult to attack.

5 Who escaped back to Scotland after the revolt of Edwin and Morcar?

6 What did the Harrying of the North involve?

7 Name three ways in which land was transferred from Anglo-Saxons to Normans.

8 Name the three earls who plotted against William in 1075.

9 What happened to each of the three earls after their revolt was defeated?

10 Who was in charge in England at the start of the Revolt of the Earls?

Exam-style question, Section B

'William's strategy for ruling England had failed by 1070'.

How far do you agree? Explain your answer.

You may use the following in your answer:

*   the submission of the earls
*   the Harrying of the North.

You **must** also use information of your own. **16 marks**

Exam tip

This question is asking you to consider points for and against the statement in order to make a judgement.

*   The hint in the first bullet point supports the statement. You could use this first to write about reasons why the statement is correct.
*   The hint in the second bullet point could be used against the statement. You could say that his strategy had not worked if he needed to punish the North so harshly.
*   Use another point of your own and say whether it supports the statement or argues against it.
*   Make sure you say whether or not you agree with the statement.

Activities

1   The spider diagram here has been started off for you – copy it out onto a large sheet of paper and complete it to detail: causes, consequences, features and characteristics.

2   What question about this topic would you like to know the answer to? For example, did Harold have any children and, if so, did they try to recover their lands? Or how important were women in Anglo-Saxon revolts? Research an answer to your question for a presentation to the rest of the class.

3   Compare the royal power of William with that of Edward the Confessor. To what extent did William continue the powers of the king rather than change them?

● Establishing control
  o   Submission of the earls
  o   Rewarding followers
  o   Marcher earldoms
  o   Why were castles important?

● How resistance changed William's rule
  o   Harrying of the North, 1069–70
  o   Changes in landownership
  o   Maintaining royal power

William in power: securing the kingdom, 1066–87

● Anglo-Saxon resistance, 1068–71
  o   Edwin and Morcar, 1068
  o   Rebellion in the North, 1069
  o   Hereward the Wake, 1070–71

● The Revolt of the Earls, 1075

Writing historically: building sentences

Successful historical writing uses a range of sentence structures to help you be as clear and precise as possible.

Learning outcomes

By the end of this lesson, you will understand how to:

- link ideas with clarity and precision
- change sentence structure to emphasise key ideas.

Definitions

Clause: a group of words that contains a verb and can form part or all of a sentence.

Single clause sentence: a sentence containing just one clause.

Subordinating conjunction: a word used to link a dependent clause to the main clause of a sentence.

Compare the two drafts of sentences below, written in response to this exam-style question:

> Explain why William was able to become king of England after the Battle of Hastings. **(12 marks)**

These points are written in pairs of unlinked, **single clause sentences**.

The connection between these points is made clear with **subordinating conjunctions**.

William's use of castle building was key to his success. It ensured his control of the areas he took.	William's castle building was key to his success **because** it ensured his control of the areas he took.
William had won the Battle of Hastings. The Witan chose Edgar Aethling to become king of England.	**Although** William had won the Battle of Hastings, the Witan chose Edgar Aethling to become king of England.
William secured the south coast. He built castles at Hastings and Dover.	**After** he secured the south coast, William built castles at Hastings and Dover.

1. Which responses are more clearly expressed? Write a sentence or two explaining your answer.

Subordinating conjunctions can link ideas to indicate:

- an explanation: (e.g. 'because', 'as', 'in order that')
- a condition: (e.g. 'if', 'unless')
- a comparison: (e.g. 'although', 'whereas')
- a sequence: (e.g. 'when', 'as', 'before', 'until' etc.).

How can I structure my sentences for clarity and emphasis?

In sentences where ideas are linked with subordinate conjunctions, there is:

- a main clause that gives the most important point of the sentence
- a follow-on, subordinate clause that adds more information about that central point.

Different sentence structures can alter the focus of your writing. Look at these sentences that have been used to introduce responses to the exam-style question on the previous page.

Compare these two versions of the first sentence:

> *Although William had won the Battle of Hastings, the Witan chose Edgar Aethling to become king of England. William's decisions and tactics enabled him to become king instead.*

This is the main clause in this sentence

This is a subordinate clause. It is linked to the main clause with <u>a subordinating conjunction.</u>

> *The Witan chose Edgar Aethling to become king of England although William had won the Battle of Hastings. William's decisions and tactics enabled him to become king instead.*

2. Which version do you prefer? Write a sentence or two explaining your decision.

In both responses, the second sentence is much shorter than the first sentence.

3.　Experiment with different ways of organising the three pieces of information in the student's response above, linking all, some, or none of them with subordinating conjunctions:

> *William had won the Battle of Hastings.*
>
> *The Witan chose Edgar Aethling to become king of England.*
>
> *William's decisions and tactics enabled him to become king instead.*

Which version do you prefer? One of yours or the original version? Write a sentence explaining your decision.

Improving an answer

4. Now look at the notes below written in response to the exam-style question on the previous page.

> *William's tactics were a key reason for his success.*
>
> *He marched on London.*
>
> *He ruthlessly harried and burned wherever he went.*
>
> *He intimidated the Anglo-Saxons.*
>
> *They felt demoralised and incapable of resistance.*
>
> *The earls submitted to him at Berkhamstead.*
>
> *William had convinced them of his military superiority.*

a. Experiment with different ways of arranging and structuring all the information in sentences. Try to write at least two different versions.

b. Which version do you prefer? Write a sentence explaining your decision.

03 | Norman England, 1066–88

How different was Norman England from Anglo-Saxon England?

Historians used to think that the feudal system introduced to England by William I was **very** different from how Anglo-Saxon society was organised. Now, historians have identified many ways in which the Norman government was similar to government under Edward the Confessor. What was most different was that the Norman government aimed to strengthen Norman control and make the king more powerful and richer.

The Domesday Book was William's record of who owned what in Norman England and how much they owed the king in taxation.

Learning outcomes

In this chapter you will find out:

- about the feudal system and changes to the Church by the Normans
- how Norman government worked and what its aims were
- about the Norman aristocracy and the importance of Bishop Odo of Bayeux
- about William I and his sons, and what happened after William died.

3.1 The feudal system and the Church

Learning outcomes

- Understand the feudal hierarchy and the nature of feudalism.
- Understand the role of the Church and its Normanisation and reform.
- Understand the extent of change to Anglo-Saxon society and economy.

The feudal system and feudal hierarchy

The feudal system was a way of making sure the king had troops without him having to pay for them.

However, keeping an army was enormously expensive. All the soldiers needed to be paid, men and horses had to be fed, equipment bought and maintained. Knights, in particular, were very expensive.

The system worked like this:

- William granted land to his tenants-in-chief to reward them for their loyalty. In return they would provide troops when the king needed them.
- Land with this service obligation was called a fief*.
- Some fiefs required the holder to provide knights for battle or to send troops to guard the king's castles.
- Knight service* was for 40 days a year and was unpaid.

If a tenant-in-chief had to provide ten knights to the king (his fief), then he could grant out ten parcels of land to ten of his knights to live on. When the king needed the knights, they would go off to fight for him.

William created a feudal hierarchy* (see Figure 3.1) with himself alone at the top.

Key terms

Fief*
Land held by a vassal in return for service to a lord. Also called a 'feud' (i.e. feudalism).

Knight service*
The duty to provide a mounted knight to the king in exchange for a grant of land. The vassal had to ensure the knight had the right armour, weapons and equipment to carry out their service.

Feudal hierarchy*
A hierarchy puts people into order according to their importance. In the feudal hierarchy, the king was at the top and peasants at the bottom.

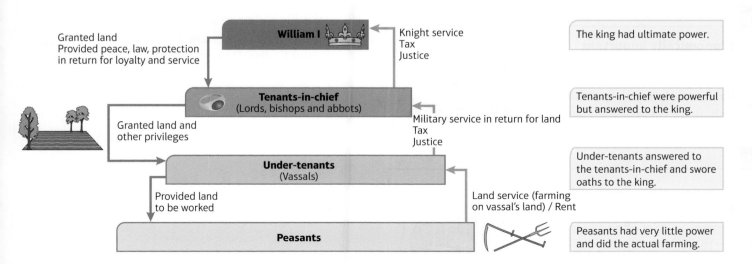

Granted land
Provided peace, law, protection in return for loyalty and service

William I

Knight service
Tax
Justice

The king had ultimate power.

Tenants-in-chief
(Lords, bishops and abbots)

Granted land and other privileges

Military service in return for land
Tax
Justice

Tenants-in-chief were powerful but answered to the king.

Under-tenants
(Vassals)

Provided land to be worked

Under-tenants answered to the tenants-in-chief and swore oaths to the king.

Land service (farming on vassal's land) / Rent

Peasants

Peasants had very little power and did the actual farming.

Figure 3.1 The feudal hierarchy of William I.

The role and importance of tenants-in-chief

- Tenants-in-chief held their fiefs direct from the king.
- They had military, social, political and economic roles.
- Some were Church leaders: bishops and abbots.

Activity ?

Whenever you are working on analysis of the Anglo-Saxons and Normans, the following five categories can help organise your thinking:

- social
- political
- economic
- military
- religious.

Use these categories and the image opposite to decide which one category you think is most important for understanding tenants-in-chief.

Military
Tenants-in-chief were expected to fight with the king and lead their own band of knights. They also had to put down any opposition to Norman rule.

Social
Tenants-in-chief decided who to give their land (fiefs) out to. They gave land to their Norman knights and took it away from Anglo-Saxons.

Social
The tenants-in-chief organised courts. These courts made judgements about who was allowed to use which bits of land.

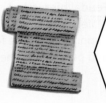

Activities ?

1. Study the information on the role and importance of tenants-in-chief. Identify what the roles of the tenants-in-chief were (using the categories of social, political, economic and military).

2. For each role of the tenant-in-chief, explain why it was important in Norman England.

3. How big a change was the feudal system compared to how society was organised in Anglo-Saxon England? Identify at least one similarity and one difference.

Economically important
Tenants-in-chief paid the king a share of all the revenue produced by their fiefs and they also kept a share for themselves. Many became extremely wealthy.

Political
Tenants-in-chief often had a role in the royal court, advising the king.

The role and importance of knight service

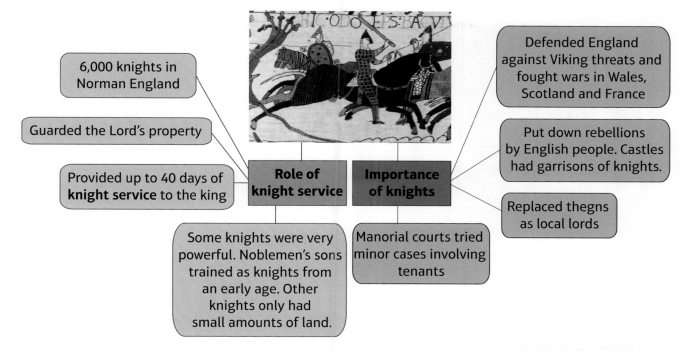

6,000 knights in Norman England

Guarded the Lord's property

Provided up to 40 days of **knight service** to the king

Some knights were very powerful. Noblemen's sons trained as knights from an early age. Other knights only had small amounts of land.

Role of knight service

Importance of knights

Defended England against Viking threats and fought wars in Wales, Scotland and France

Put down rebellions by English people. Castles had garrisons of knights.

Replaced thegns as local lords

Manorial courts tried minor cases involving tenants

► Knight service meant William could call up knights from all his tenants-in-chief.

The nature of feudalism

Landholding

Anglo-Saxon landholding was very complex. William's feudal system was much simpler. The King owned all the land.

- In Anglo-Saxon England, many people had owned their land and were able to pass it on to their heirs.
- In Norman England, when a landholder died, the heir had to pay the king for the right to use the land. This payment was called a **relief.**

Reliefs encouraged loyalty to the king in three main ways.

- The king could decide how much the relief should be. That meant he could reward his most loyal followers by saying their family only needed to pay small reliefs.
- The king could punish landholders by setting such a high relief that their heir would struggle to pay it.
- When a new heir took over the land, they had to do homage* to the king. Breaking this promise would be a very bad thing to do.

Reliefs also annoyed the Normans. Normans wanted to build up their power and pass it on to their sons. Reliefs could stop this happening.

Key term

Homage*

To demonstrate loyalty to another person publically.

Source A

Knights defend a castle from attack – an important part of knight service. From a 12th century bible.

▶ The homage ceremony continued throughout the medieval period.

Homage

When William granted land to a tenant-in-chief, an important ceremony of homage took place.

- The baron knelt before the king, put his hands between the king's hands and said: 'I become your man.'
- The baron then placed his hand on the Bible and promised to remain faithful for the rest of his life.

- The tenant-in-chief carried out the same kind of ceremonies with his tenants.

Labour service

Labour service was about working the lord's lands in return for the use of land.

Often these jobs involved ploughing the lord's fields, sowing the lord's crops and harvesting them when they had grown.

Other common forms of labour service were to provide a certain amount of goods each year; for example, a set amount of honey from beehives or eels from rivers.

Forfeiture

Forfeiture was the punishment for not carrying out land service or knight service – having the land you used taken away from you. Sometimes people might be punished with a fine instead.

The Church in England

The Church's social roles and connection to government

The Church in Norman England was important for social reasons as well as for religious ones.

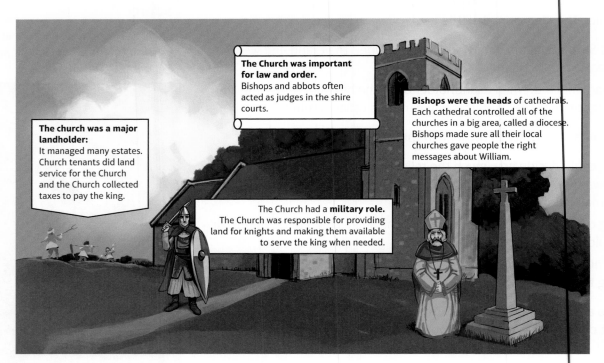

The church was a major landholder: It managed many estates. Church tenants did land service for the Church and the Church collected taxes to pay the king.

The Church was important for law and order. Bishops and abbots often acted as judges in the shire courts.

The Church had a **military role.** The Church was responsible for providing land for knights and making them available to serve the king when needed.

Bishops were the heads of cathedrals. Each cathedral controlled all of the churches in a big area, called a diocese. Bishops made sure all their local churches gave people the right messages about William.

Figure 3.2 The Church's social roles.

The Church was also closely connected to Norman government.

- Bishops and abbots were well-educated and were often valuable advisers to the king.
- Bishops often helped make laws for the king and gave him legal advice.
- Church clerks sent out the king's writs and looked after the royal seal (see page 15).
- Archbishop Lanfranc acted as William's regent* while the king was in Normandy.

At first, William kept on many Anglo-Saxon Church leaders: for example he was crowned by Ealdred, Archbishop of York. He wanted them to say he was the legitimate heir of Edward the Confessor, and was ruling England as Edward had done.

But after the rebellions of 1068–70, William replaced almost all the Anglo-Saxon Church leaders with his own men. For example, in 1070, Stigand, the Archbishop of Canterbury, was replaced by Lanfranc.

Key term

Regent*

Someone appointed to act for a king or queen when they are underage or unable to rule because of illness or being out of the country.

Comparing the roles of Stigand and Lanfranc

Archbishop Lanfranc had many of the same roles as Stigand. But there were also important differences.

Roles Stigand and Lanfranc had in common
- Both served on the the royal council (Witan) – advising the king.
- Both acted as the king's representative.
- Both were legal experts and helped the king understand the law and write new laws.
- Both were administrators: organising Church business.
- Both were tenants-in-chief and helped the king defend his kingdom.

Roles for Lanfranc only
- Head of the Church in England – Stigand did not control all of England.
- Reforming the Church – modernising England's Church.
- Rebuilding churches – knocking down Anglo-Saxon churches and building Norman ones.
- Reinforcing Norman control of England.

Figure 3.3 Roles Stigand and Lanfranc had in common.

Lanfranc's reform of the Church

Lanfranc was a reformer. He wanted to change the Church.

- Instead of the Church thinking of ways to make money, Lanfranc thought the Church should think about only religion.
- Instead of priests getting married, Lanfranc thought they should not have sexual relationships, and focus on God instead.
- Lanfranc banned marriage for priests and made celibacy (having no sexual relationships at all) compulsory for priests. (Priests who were already married could stay married.)
- Anglo-Saxon cathedrals out in the countryside were knocked down and rebuilt in towns (for example: Sherborne to Salisbury). This meant the bishop of the cathedral was now in a more secure location with more control over his area.
- Lanfranc increased the number of monasteries in England, especially in the North. He was a strong supporter of monasteries because in Norman monasteries, monks lived a pure and religious life.

Normanisation and the Church

Within 50 years of 1066, every English church, cathedral and most abbeys had been demolished and rebuilt in Norman style.

Anglo-Saxon Church leaders also lost their jobs so that, after 1070, there was only one remaining Anglo-Saxon bishop – Wulfstan, bishop of Worcester. Changing the Church to be more Norman is called 'Normanisation'. Normanisation meant that the Church was used to strengthen Norman control over England.

- Norman bishops and archdeacons made sure local churches told people how amazing William and the Normans were.
- The Church owned one quarter of all land in England. Installing loyal Normans as bishops and archbishops secured these lands against possible Anglo-Saxon rebellions.
- Lanfranc's reforms meant that parish priests came under stricter Church control and were made to follow Norman Church procedures and customs.

Lanfranc's to-do list

Church reform in England

- ✓ No more marriage or relationships for priests (focus on God).
- ✓ Church to be more spiritual and less about making money!
- ✓ Move remote cathedrals into towns (to keep an eye on things).
- ✓ More monasteries – with very pure lifestyles for the monks.

Important changes under Lanfranc

Church reform in England

- ✓ More power. The Archbishop of Canterbury to be made the head of the church in England. This means Lanfranc can enforce his reforms.
- ✓ End church corruption. Stigand was bishop of both Canterbury and Winchester (being bishop of more than one area was called **pluralism**). Stigand also sold church jobs for money (this was called **simony**). Lafranc was against both of these.

▶ Lanfranc was a reformer who wanted to change the Church.

The Normanised Church enhanced the king's power:

- New bishops did homage to the king – they had to swear loyalty to him.
- The king oversaw Church councils and his approval was needed for key decisions.
- Church leaders who failed their obligations could forfeit their lands.
- When a bishop died, the king appointed his successor.

Exam-style question, Section B

'The main consequence of the Normanisation of England was that the king became more powerful'.

How far do you agree? Explain your answer.

You may use the following in your answer:

- the feudal system
- Archbishop Lanfranc.

You **must** also use information of your own. **16 marks**

Exam tip

You could use the following sentence starters in your answer:

- Normanisation meant the feudal system put the king in charge of everyone's land. This gave him more power because he could use reliefs to…
- Getting rid of thegns and replacing them with Norman knights meant more power for the king because…

Also think of another consequence that is not about the king's power (Hint: think about changes in the church).

The extent of change

Landholding was the basis of society and the economy. William's imposition of the feudal system looks like a huge change to the Anglo-Saxon way of life. But was it?

Anglo-Saxon society

 Slaves made up around 10% of the population.

 Peasants made up around 80% of the population. Some were free peasants.

 4,000–6,000 thegns: local landowners who provided military services to their lords.

 Some earls were so powerful and wealthy that they posed a threat to the king.

Norman society

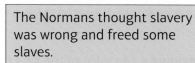 The Normans thought slavery was wrong and freed some slaves.

 Feudalism bound peasants to their lords. Norman lords may have worked peasants harder. But this was not a huge change.

 Thegns wiped out as a landowning class and replaced by knights and other Norman vassals of tenants-in-chief.

 Earls replaced by Normans and earldoms made much smaller. Earls were tenants-in-chief, dependent on the king.

▶ Differences between Anglo-Saxon and Norman society.

THINKING HISTORICALLY — Cause and Consequence (3c&d)

Causation and intention

1 Identify as many causes for the development of feudalism in Norman England as you can. Write each cause on a separate card or piece of paper.

2 Divide your cards into:

   a what people did (actions)

   b what people believed (beliefs).

3 Focus on the beliefs and actions of William and Lanfranc in the development of feudalism after the Norman Conquest. Use your knowledge to fill in a table, identifying:

   a what they wanted in 1066

   b what they did to achieve what they wanted

   c the consequences of their actions

   d whether they got what they wanted.

Continuity

Continuity means when things **stay the same**. Some parts of England showed more continuity than change after the Norman conquest.

For example, in the villages, life for most peasants would have continued much as it had before.

Another example of continuity was the royal household.

For example, the roles of the king's personal servants, troops, clerks and advisors didn't change. What did change was that William gave these roles to his Norman followers.

Most important of all to William must have been the **geld tax**.

- The Norman's didn't have a geld tax.
- William used it more often than Edward had.
- He used this Anglo-Saxon tax to take money from the Anglo-Saxons for himself and his Norman supporters.

Change

One of the biggest changes for Anglo-Saxons must have been **castle-building** and the rebuilding of churches and cathedrals in stone.

For example, large areas of some towns were cleared to make room for the new, very Norman, castles and cathedrals.

Anglo-Saxon England had traded widely, including with Scandinavian countries. Under the Normans, trade with Scandinavia went down, but trade with Normandy went up.

This meant many big English cities became much larger under the Normans.

William changed a lot of England's social roles as well.

- Tenants-in-chief had many of the same roles as earls, but the king had much stronger control over tenants-in-chief – for example, reliefs, homage and forfeiture. William did this to try and prevent men gathering enough power to challenge him as king.

- Thegns were replaced by knights. These were Normans who depended on their tenants-in-chief for land and who owed knight service to the king.

- The feudal system meant that most knights were much less independent than thegns.

- Their tenants-in-chief had much greater control over them if they did not fulfil their obligations.

- Most knights were quite poor and the service they did for the king involved guarding his castles, not heroic battles against Viking invaders.

Because Anglo-Saxon England was much richer and more sophisticated than Normandy, the Normans took on lots of English ways of doing things.

The things William changed were meant to give him and the Normans control over the economy and prevent Anglo-Saxon resistance.

▶ This Norman castle is in Dover. The Normans used their castles to spread their power.

3.1 The feudal system and the Church: summary

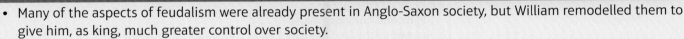

- Many of the aspects of feudalism were already present in Anglo-Saxon society, but William remodelled them to give him, as king, much greater control over society.
- Lanfranc's reforms of the Church were inspired by European reforms, but they worked to increase Norman control over England rather than allow the pope to challenge William's power.
- William was keen to use Anglo-Saxon roles and practices that helped Norman control over England. Sometimes this could be achieved by replacing Anglo-Saxons with Normans. Sometimes, bigger changes were required.

Checkpoint

Strengthen

S1 Identify two ways in which Lanfranc changed the Church in England.

S2 Describe two ways in which the feudal system of Norman England was different from how society had worked under Edward the Confessor.

Challenge

C1 Develop a comparison chart that identifies change and continuity between Anglo-Saxon England and Norman England under William I. Consider: the power of the king, landholding, the Church's influence, towns and villages, and the military.

How confident do you feel about your answers to these questions? If you are not sure that you answered them well, try the activity on page 76.

Learning outcomes

- Understand the changes to government brought in by William.
- Understand the office of sheriff and the demesne, the introduction of the 'forest'.
- Understand the creation and significance of the Domesday Book.

Continuity in government

England had much more advanced government than Normandy. William chose to keep what worked. He then adapted these government systems so they increased the power of the king and took more money from the English economy. For example:

- Norman government used the hide for working out tax payments, like the Anglo-Saxons had done, and kept the shire and the hundred (see page 14).

- William kept the Witan. When Norman England was facing Danish invasion in 1085, William gathered all the important landholders together in a large-scale Witan.

- The Norman economy used the Anglo-Saxon system of silver pennies and the royal treasury remained at Winchester, although William kept an even tighter control on who was allowed to mint coins.

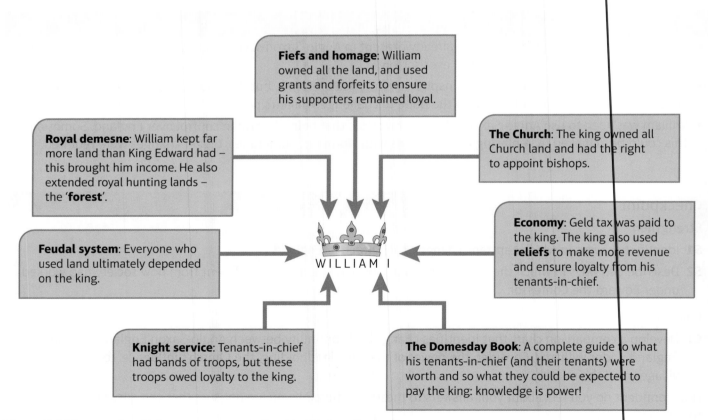

Fiefs and homage: William owned all the land, and used grants and forfeits to ensure his supporters remained loyal.

Royal demesne: William kept far more land than King Edward had – this brought him income. He also extended royal hunting lands – the **'forest'**.

The Church: The king owned all Church land and had the right to appoint bishops.

Feudal system: Everyone who used land ultimately depended on the king.

Economy: Geld tax was paid to the king. The king also used **reliefs** to make more revenue and ensure loyalty from his tenants-in-chief.

WILLIAM I

Knight service: Tenants-in-chief had bands of troops, but these troops owed loyalty to the king.

The Domesday Book: A complete guide to what his tenants-in-chief (and their tenants) were worth and so what they could be expected to pay the king: knowledge is power!

Figure 3.4 The ways in which power was centralised in Norman England.

Changes in government

Centralised power

William centralised power in his hands. He owned all the land and used fiefs to reward followers and forfeits to punish anyone who acted against him.

In Anglo-Saxon England, the earls had sometimes challenged the king. This had caused Edward the Confessor problems, for example:

- Edward had to depend on other earls' support when he wanted to exile Earl Godwin in 1051.
- Edward the Confessor had wanted the earls to lead an army against the Northumbrian rebels in 1065, but the earls had made excuses not to.

Reduced role of earls
- William made the earldoms smaller and more compact, or got rid of them altogether (Wessex and Mercia, for example).
- The special powers given to the Marcher earls immediately after the conquest were reduced.
- Earls were tenants-in-chief and subject to the same requirements as William's other barons.
- Some heirs of earldoms resented these changes, like in the Revolt of the Earls in 1075.

The role of regents
Because William had two countries to run he relied on regents. William only used his most trusted followers as his regents.

However, William tended to return as soon as he heard of trouble in England. Perhaps this was because of the problems caused by his first two regents, Odo of Bayeux and William FitzOsbern. Their greedy and violent actions in 1067 helped cause Anglo-Saxon resistance.

Key term
Demesne*
The land that the king or a tenant kept for his own use rather than granting it as a fief to an under-tenant. It is pronounced 'de-mean'.

Exam-style question, Section B	
Describe **two** features of Norman government.
4 marks

Exam tip	
This question is about features. Make sure you identify two and add information about each of them.
Here are some features you could consider using:

- the Witan
- earls/the Marcher earls
- sheriffs
- geld tax.

The office of the sheriff and the demesne

In Edward the Confessor's reign, the shire reeve (or sheriff, for short) had these main roles:

- He was the king's representative. The sheriff collected the money owed to the king from the shires and towns. He also looked after the king's own lands, called his demesne*.
- The sheriff was the earl's representative. He was responsible for law and order in his shire. The sheriff was also responsible for making sure his shire had good defences and that it had men for the fyrd.

Sheriffs in Norman England
After the Conquest, the sheriff's two main roles stayed very similar to how they had been before. But William changed the people doing the job: replacing Anglo-Saxons with Normans. Sheriffs were almost all Normans by 1071.

Some Anglo-Saxon sheriffs had joined the rebellions against Norman rule (for example, Maerleswein in Yorkshire), so replacing them with loyal followers would have been a priority for William.

Resentment against sheriffs

There were also some changes to the role of sheriff under the Normans:

- Sheriffs could keep a share of the money they collected for the king. They also kept some of the money paid in fines to the shire courts. This meant sheriffs could make a lot of money for themselves if they wanted to really squeeze the locals.

- Sheriffs were often involved in land-grabs following the Conquest. Because of their power, there was no one to complain to except the king.

- These actions made Norman sheriffs very unpopular with the Anglo-Saxons in their shire.

	Anglo-Saxon sheriffs	Norman sheriffs
Importance	The king appointed the sheriffs, but the sheriff was less important than his earl. Sheriffs had to be careful not to upset their earl.	• The sheriff was still appointed by the king, but now the role had much **greater** power. • Sheriffs answered to nobody but the king. • Norman sheriffs were very important men. The king required them to keep close control over their shires and those who failed him forfeited their role.
Law and order	Sheriffs were responsible for maintaining law and order in their shire. Sheriffs were in charge of the shire court.	The Normans **kept** the same legal system, but added new laws to punish rebellion against Norman control, which the sheriff was also responsible for enforcing.
Defence	The sheriff was responsible for the defence of his shire: for keeping roads and defences well-maintained and for gathering together the fyrd when the king needed it.	• Sheriffs **kept** the role of organising the defence of the shire and gathering together the fyrd, but this system now ran alongside knight service, which the sheriff was not responsible for. • The sheriff's main military role was usually as custodian of the king's castles in the shire.

The introduction and significance of the 'forest'

An important part of the sheriff's role in maintaining law and order in Norman England was capturing and punishing anyone who broke forest law.

The introduction of the 'forest'

- Early medieval kings loved hunting, and William was especially keen on hunting.
- In Anglo-Saxon England, the king was free to hunt wherever he wanted to across his own lands. William made new areas into 'forest', taking them away from other landholders.
- Forest land was not necessarily covered in trees, it meant land that was reserved for hunting by the king and protected from other uses by law.
- Whole regions became 'forest', including the New Forest in southern England.
- Chroniclers at the time report large numbers of families being thrown out of their homes as their land was reclassified as 'forest'.

Forest laws

Forest laws were introduced, protecting the animals that were best to hunt, for example deer and boar. Laws to protect animals included:

- no hunting weapons in the 'forest'
- no hunting dogs in the 'forest'.

There were restrictions on cutting wood, clearing land and constructing buildings in the 'forest'.

- This made life difficult for people living within the 'forest', who depended on woodland for fuel and timber for construction, used dogs for herding animals (and as companions) and hunted rabbits and birds for food.

Activities ?

1. Identify two ways in which the role of sheriff under William changed from the role under Edward the Confessor.

2. Create a spider diagram of the ways in which the introduction of forest laws affected ordinary people living in forest areas. Were there any benefits (think of jobs that might be created)?

3. Write a conversation between two Anglo-Saxons who live an area that's just become 'forest' – they could be complaining about their sheriff.

The significance of the 'forest'

- It showed the power of the king to be above everything else.

- Extending the forest increased the amount of land the king controlled directly.

- Harsh punishments for breaking forest laws show the brutal side of Norman rule. Contemporary sources say people who killed William's deer for food were blinded.

- All the fines paid by those breaking forest laws brought in more money for the king.

Ordinary people thought it was unfair that animals were given protection while people went hungry.

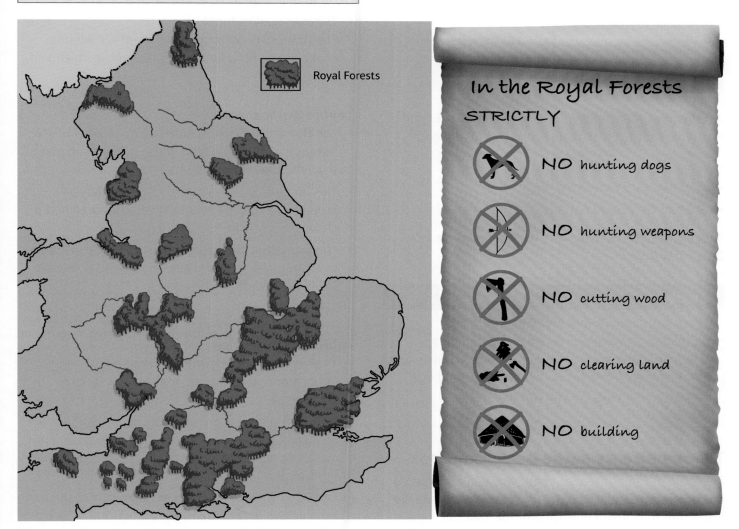

Figure 3.5 Map of royal forest lands as of c1200, when the forest was at its greatest extent.

The Domesday Book and its significance

Source A

The Anglo-Saxon Chronicle for 1085 describes the way the Domesday Book data was collected.

The king sent his men over all England into every shire and had them find out how many hundred hides there were in the shire, or what land and cattle the king himself had in the country, or what dues he ought to have in twelve months from the shire. Also he had a record made of how much [...] everybody had who was occupying land in England, in land or cattle, and how much money it was worth.

Timeline

William's last years

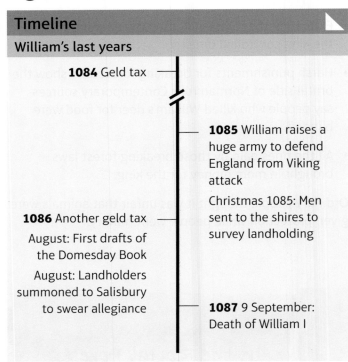

1084 Geld tax

1085 William raises a huge army to defend England from Viking attack

Christmas 1085: Men sent to the shires to survey landholding

1086 Another geld tax

August: First drafts of the Domesday Book

August: Landholders summoned to Salisbury to swear allegiance

1087 9 September: Death of William I

At Christmas 1085, William ordered a survey of England. Men were sent to investigate each shire to find out:

- who held what land
- what taxes they owed the king
- whether they could pay any more.

The results of this survey were written up in the Domesday Book.

Activity ?

Access translated Domesday Book records for your region (or a region you are interested in) at www.opendomesday.org. Working as a class, discover who the tenants-in-chief were, how much geld was owed and what changes you can find between 1066 and 1086.

The significance of the Domesday Book

There are different theories about why William ordered the Domesday Book to be put together. It was certainly important to Norman government for financial, legal and military reasons.

Financial significance

- One reason for the Domesday Book was money. William wanted to find out how much more he could get from his tenants.
- The king made a lot of money from charging reliefs. The Domesday Book helped William see what he could charge for reliefs when a tenant-in-chief died.

Legal significance

- The Domesday Book includes many cases of Anglo-Saxons claiming that land of theirs had been taken from them by Normans.
- The Domesday surveys were made as fairly as possible. All the key people in each hundred had a chance to say who really owned what.
- The Domesday Book helped sort out legal disputes over land. William may have wanted this so people in England could see he was a fair king.

Military significance

- The main reason why William called a council in December 1085 was to discuss a new Viking invasion threat.
- Although the invasion never happened, William took the threat seriously. He brought thousands of soldiers over from Normandy. These soldiers joined the troops of landholders all over England.
- The Domesday Book may have been part of this preparation to see how many soldiers each Tenant-in-chief could provide.

Exam-style question, Section B

'The main significance of the Domesday Book was financial'. How far do you agree? Explain your answer.

You may use the following in your answer:

- invasion threats
- the geld tax.

You **must** also use information of your own. **16 marks**

Exam tip

This question is about significance. Even if you think the Domesday Book **was** all about money (financial), you still need to show **why** money was more important than its other significant impacts. Source B suggests some points you could use in your answer.

Source B

The Domesday Book was compiled from detailed surveys made in (at least) seven regions. The photo shown here is of pages for Suffolk.

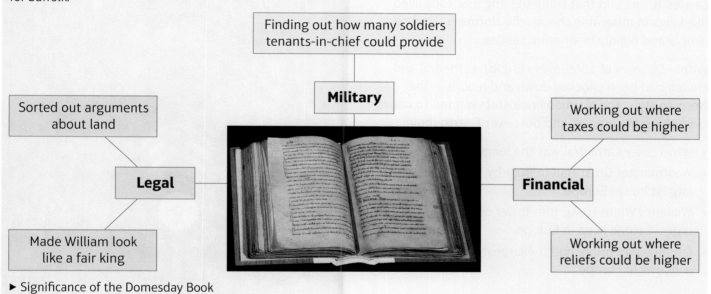

Finding out how many soldiers tenants-in-chief could provide

Military

Sorted out arguments about land

Legal

Made William look like a fair king

Working out where taxes could be higher

Financial

Working out where reliefs could be higher

▶ Significance of the Domesday Book

3.2 Norman government: summary

- The Normans kept many Anglo-Saxon systems, but William centralised power so that no one responsible for English government had enough wealth or power to challenge his rule.
- The sheriff was the king's representative in the shire. William strengthened the sheriff's authority as part of the centralisation of power.
- The Domesday Book was a tool for William's central control. The detailed landholding surveys allowed William to see what money and duties his tenants-in-chief owed in almost every area of his kingdom.

Checkpoint

Strengthen

S1 Was William a fair or unfair king? Use an example to back up your answer.

S2 Describe two ways in which the role of the sheriff changed after the Norman Conquest.

Challenge

C1 Identify three ways in which William centralised government roles in England to increase his own power.

3.3 The Norman aristocracy

Culture

Anglo-Saxon aristocrats showed off with rich clothes and jewels, and gave each other expensive gifts. The Norman aristocrats did not do this. They put their money into building impressive new churches, cathedrals and castles. It was said that while the Anglo-Saxons lived like kings in miserable shacks, the Normans lived very simply and plainly in amazing castles.

Within 50 years of 1066, every English cathedral and church had been knocked down and rebuilt in the Norman style. The Norman aristocrats wanted to make everything the biggest and best ever. For example:

- Winchester Cathedral was the longest in Europe.
- Westminster Great Hall (rebuilt by William II) was the largest hall in Europe.
- William's White Tower (the Tower of London) was the biggest stone keep in Europe.
- Canterbury's priory had the largest stained-glass windows in Europe.

Source A

The interior of Durham Cathedral still has lots of Norman features. Building work began in 1093.

Anglo-Saxon aristocrats showed off their wealth with rich clothes and expensive jewellery

Norman aristocrats wore simple clothes and put their wealth into fancy stone buildings

▶ Norman aristocrats showed off their wealth very differently from Anglo-Saxon aristocrats.

Christian culture

Norman aristocrats were very religious. They believed they must do penance* for their actions in battle.

All those Normans who fought against the English at Hastings, for example, were ordered to do a year of penance for each man killed; 40 days' penance for each man wounded and, if they weren't sure how many English they had killed, they should build a church.

By praying, doing penance and giving money to the Church, Norman aristocrats hoped to avoid going to Hell when they died.

Attitudes to the English

The Normans did not think very much of the English. They did not respect English religious traditions and they were rude about the English.

- The Normans threw away holy items from Anglo-Saxon churches. They often destroyed the tombs of Anglo-Saxon church leaders and called these holy men 'idiots'.
- The Normans used the word 'English' as an insult. One Norman called going to the toilet 'doing an English'.

Language

Few Normans bothered to learn English:

- William tried to learn English, so he could understand land claims better, but had to give up because he didn't have time.
- When Lanfranc was made archbishop in 1070, he couldn't speak English.
- Written English was almost completely replaced by Latin for documents, while the aristocracy talked to each other in French.
- Norman aristocrats probably never needed to worry about learning English at all because they used interpreters to talk to English people.
- At the same time, many Norman aristocrats didn't understand Latin any better than English, so they wouldn't have understood the king's writs sent to them until they were translated into French by their clerks.

Key term

Penance*

Penance meant saying sorry to God through prayer and religious actions. For example, fasting: not eating for a day or more.

▶ William paid for this abbey to be built near the scene of the Battle of Hastings. It is likely that he did this as his penance for the men he killed in the battle against Harold.

Activities

1. Think about ways in which people show off status today, especially in music videos full of fast cars, jewellery, amazing houses and attractive party-goers. Storyboard what a Norman aristocrat would include in their bragging music video.

2. Write a diary entry for a Norman aristocrat observing life on the streets from their castle window. How would they have described the English people they saw below them?

3. Explain why the Normans felt bad about winning battles when they spent so many years training to be warriors.

Career and significance of Bishop Odo

Timeline

The career of Bishop Odo

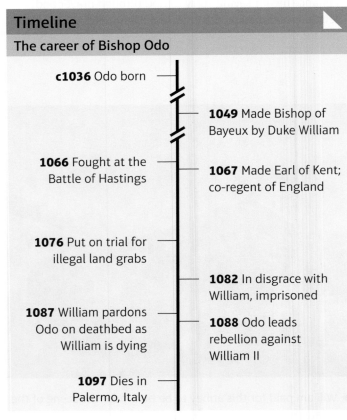

c1036 Odo born

1049 Made Bishop of Bayeux by Duke William

1066 Fought at the Battle of Hastings

1067 Made Earl of Kent; co-regent of England

1076 Put on trial for illegal land grabs

1082 In disgrace with William, imprisoned

1087 William pardons Odo on deathbed as William is dying

1088 Odo leads rebellion against William II

1097 Dies in Palermo, Italy

Source B

Bishop Odo as portrayed in the Bayeux Tapestry. He is the one with the club. It is thought that Odo ordered the Tapestry to be made.

Odo and the Conquest

Odo was William's half-brother: they had the same mother, Herleva. In 1049, William made Odo Bishop of Bayeux, even though Odo had a bad reputation. Odo was a major supporter of William's invasion, giving 100 ships to the fleet. He fought at the Battle of Hastings (see Source B).

William rewarded him with the earldom of Kent as well as so much other land that Odo became the second largest landholder in England, after the king.

Significance

- William's most trusted supporters were his family members. They were rewarded richly.

- Odo's bad reputation (he was greedy and immoral) did not stop William from giving him important positions. William's first priority was loyalty.

Odo and power

Odo was co-regent during William's first absence in 1067. During his time as regent, Odo:

- built castles across his lands
- treated the English people very badly
- took the law into his own hands, for example deciding court cases himself, as if he was king.

Odo is described as 'dreaded by Englishmen everywhere, and able to dispense justice like a second king'.

Significance

- Odo (and co-regent FitzOsbern) seem to have wrecked the king's attempts to gain Anglo-Saxon acceptance of his reign with their violent and oppressive actions as co-regents.

- King William allowed Odo a lot of power; he was able to act as 'a second king'.

Odo in trouble

The Domesday Book records page after page of complaints against Odo for illegally seizing land, including Church land in Canterbury.

In the end, it was Lanfranc who complained about Odo to William. A three-day investigation in 1076 made Odo hand back the Church's land.

In 1079, William sent Odo to Northumberland. This was because there had been attacks from Scotland and the Bishop of Durham had been murdered.

Odo laid waste to the region. He also stole cathedral treasures, and robbed everyone he could.

In 1082, William put Odo in prison. He was only released (in 1087) when Odo's brother convinced William, who was dying, to pardon Odo.

Historians are not sure how Odo got into such trouble. It might have been his corrupt behaviour or perhaps he was trying to get the throne for himself. Most historians think it was because Odo tried to take some knights out of England with him for a journey to Rome. Taking knights from England went directly against William's idea that all knights only owed duty to him. No tenant-in-chief could be allowed to start putting together their own army, even if he was the half-brother of the king.

In 1088, Odo led many barons in revolt against William II (see page 97). This suggests that the cause of his problems with William I might have been that he wanted more and more power.

Significance

- Odo went too far in his abuse of power (in the end), but probably only because he made an enemy of Lanfranc: it isn't likely that many Anglo-Saxons who lost land to Odo ever got any back.

- If Odo was imprisoned because of taking knights from William, that shows how seriously William took the idea that knights were loyal only to him, the king.

- The pope reprimanded (told off) William for imprisoning one of his bishops: Odo. William rejected the right of the pope to criticise what he did in his own kingdom.

3.3 The Norman aristocracy: summary

- Anglo-Saxon aristocratic culture was replaced by Norman aristocratic culture.
- French took over as the language spoken by the aristocracy. Only common people spoke English.
- As a favourite of the king, Odo was untouchable. When he became a potential rival to William, all that changed.

Checkpoint

Strengthen

S1 Describe two features of Norman aristocratic culture.

S2 How does studying the story of Bishop Odo help you understand more about Norman England?

Challenge

C1 What evidence would you use to support the argument that William protected Odo while he was useful to him, but then stopped protecting him once Odo became a threat?

How confident do you feel about your answers to these questions? If you are not sure that you answered them well, try the following study skills activity.

Activity ?

It is important to use facts and evidence correctly to support a clear argument, but another key skill is using your historical imagination: this can help you connect to the topics. Back up your theories with as much factual evidence as you can. Try to imagine yourself in Odo's position in 1082. What might he have thought about his situation?

Learning outcomes

- Understand the character and personality of William and his relations with Robert.
- Understand the reasons for and outcome of the disputed succession.

The character and personality of William I

A stern, brutal and greedy man

Source A

The Anglo-Saxon Chronicle for 1087 provides an obituary (an article reporting someone's death) of William. It was written in Peterborough by a monk: we do not know much about who he was.

William was so stern and relentless a man that no one dared to cross him. Earls who resisted him were held as prisoners. Bishops and abbots lost their jobs, while he threw rebellious thegns into prison. Finally his own brother he did not spare. His name was Odo. He was master of England when the king was in Normandy. William put him in prison.

William's toughness and determination must always have been part of his character.

- He was the illegitimate* son of Duke Robert of Normandy, who made him his heir.
- When Duke Robert died in 1035, William was only around eight. He survived several assassination attempts by rivals as he grew up.
- Once he could lead his own armies, he was constantly at war, strengthening his control of Normandy.
- By 1066, he had a decade's experience of war, leadership, planning and military strategy.
- He built a brotherhood of loyal supporters.

As well as being stern and relentless, William was criticised for his greed – his love of money and treasure, and his desire to own everything.

Key term

Illegitimate*
Someone whose father and mother were not married.

Source B

Norman chronicler William of Malmesbury, from his book *The Deeds of English Kings*, written c1125.

The only thing for which William can be blamed was his anxiety for having money. William looked for any opportunity for scraping money together, he didn't care how. I have no excuse to offer, except that through dread of his enemies he used to drain the country of money with which to deter or repel them. If strength failed, he could buy off his enemies with gold. This disgraceful calamity is still happening so that both towns and churches are forced to make payments.

A devoted husband, a religious king

- William was very religious. He worked on Church reform with Lanfranc and founded (set up) abbeys.
- He is supposed to have repented (said sorry to God) on his deathbed.
- William took the English throne by force, but he always wanted to be accepted as the heir of Edward the Confessor. He wanted to be a legitimate king.
- He was devoted to his wife, Matilda. When she died in 1083, he was said to have wept for days. He trusted Matilda: she was his regent in Normandy many times.

Source C

Orderic Vitalis was a Norman monk writing around 40 years after William's death, and was certainly not present at William's deathbed. He claims to record William's last words as being:

I've persecuted the natives of England beyond all reason. I have cruelly oppressed them and unfairly taken away land from them, killed countless thousands by famine or the sword and become the barbarous murderer of many thousands both young and old of that fine race of people.

Relationship with his son, Robert

William and Matilda had at least nine children. The eldest was Robert, who was born around 1051. He was nicknamed Robert Curthose, which means 'short stockings' or 'dumpy legs'. Although Robert was a good warrior, William did not think he was ready to take control of Normandy in the 1070s. That was because Normandy was facing a lot of threats from its neighbours. There was tension between William and Robert.

In 1077, Robert's younger brothers William and Henry played a prank on Robert. They dumped water on his head. Robert was furious and a real fight started, which their father had to break up. Robert was angry his father did not punish his brothers.

In a fury, Robert took his men and tried to take over Rouen castle. When William came to arrest them, they ran away.

After William led troops against Robert and his men, Robert fled to Flanders. Then King Philip of France, William's enemy, gave Robert a castle to use on Normandy's borders, from which Robert led raids on Normandy, forcing William to raise an army against him.

Matilda had been sending money to her son behind William's back. When William found out, he was furious, although Matilda explained herself by saying that she would give her life for her children.

At a battle in 1079, Robert and William fought against each other. Robert knocked William off his horse and wounded him. With William defenceless on the ground, Robert gave his father his own horse and ordered him to retreat from the battle. This was a huge humiliation for William.

Matilda organised a meeting between William and Robert at Easter, 1080, so they could make up. William made Robert his chosen heir for Normandy again.

Activities

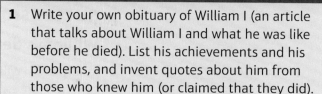

1 Write your own obituary of William I (an article that talks about William I and what he was like before he died). List his achievements and his problems, and invent quotes about him from those who knew him (or claimed that they did).

2 Pick one of the following questions about William and discuss how you would answer it. These are not questions that anyone knows the answer to for certain.

   a Did Edward the Confessor really promise William the crown?

   b Why did William commission the Domesday Book?

   c Was William truly religious, or was he only interested in what the Church could do for him?

3 In 1080, the pope wrote to Robert with some advice about the duties of a son to obey their father. Write your own version of this letter, using your knowledge of William's character and the events of 1077–80 to help you.

Source D

The tomb of Robert Curthose, in Gloucester Cathedral.

William's death and the disputed succession

William's death and funeral

In July 1087, William led a raid into France, burning down the castle and town of Mantes. By this point in his life, William had grown very fat and, when his horse stumbled, he was thrown heavily against his saddle, causing internal injuries.

William then suffered for many weeks before dying on 9 September.

The moment he died, panic broke out. His barons rode away to their castles to get ready for any attack. William's servants stole everything they could, including the furniture. They even stripped the clothes off William, leaving his naked corpse on the floor.

William's funeral was a terrible event. As William's body was put into its stone tomb, his body burst open. The terrible smell drove everyone out of the cathedral. People said this meant that God was still angry at William for his many sins.

The succession

Before he died, William decided that Robert should become Duke of Normandy after him (to succeed him), despite all the trouble between them. In 1066, all the Norman barons had sworn their allegiance to Robert as William's heir. William hoped he could trust the Norman barons to keep this promise.

William wanted his favourite son, William Rufus, to be king of England. But he was frightened that God was angry with him for the violent way he became king of England. He said he would let God choose the next king of England.

William Rufus and the defeat of Robert and Odo

William Rufus left for England before his father's death. 'Rufus' was a nickname: it means red in Latin; probably, William had red hair or red cheeks. He took with him a letter to Lanfranc from his father, recommending him as king.

Lanfranc backed him up and William Rufus was crowned William II in September 1087 at Westminster.

This suggests that Lanfranc was very powerful in England at this time: no one else needed to agree that William could be king.

Source E

William I as portrayed in the Bayeux Tapestry. Apart from the Tapestry, no portraits of William survive from his lifetime. Either side of William are his half brothers Odo and Robert of Mortain.

Odo and rebellion

Robert Curthose, as eldest son, wanted England **and** Normandy. In Norman tradition, eldest sons inherited all their father's lands.

Many Norman barons wanted the same lord in both countries, so they would not have different demands from different lords.

In 1087, Bishop Odo had been freed from prison. In 1088, he led a rebellion against William II. He wanted Robert to be king of England. Odo thought Robert would be a weak king who he and the other barons could control. William was much more like his father and would try to reduce the barons' power.

Other rebellions broke out in 1088:

- Small rebellions by Roger Bigod in Norwich and the sheriff of Leicester, Hugh de Grandmesnil; raids in Somerset and Wiltshire by Robert de Mowbray, Earl of Northumberland and in Gloucestershire by William of Eu.
- Medium-sized rebellions in the West, led by the Marcher earls Roger de Montgomery and Roger de Lacy, which were put down by a force assembled by Bishop Wulfstan (as in 1075).

However, most Norman aristocrats, bishops and also the English population were against Odo's rebellion.

- Odo and Robert of Mortain retreated to Pevensey Castle.
- William Rufus besieged the castle for six weeks. He used local fyrd troops to attack the castle and prevent any supplies reaching the rebels inside.
- His tactics worked and he captured both his uncles, though Odo then escaped to Rochester Castle.

Exam-style question, Section B

Explain why William Rufus was able to defeat the rebellion of 1088.

You may use the following in your answer:

- Bishop Odo
- the Church in England.

You **must** also use information of your own. **12 marks**

Exam tip
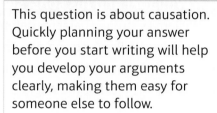

This question is about causation. Quickly planning your answer before you start writing will help you develop your arguments clearly, making them easy for someone else to follow.

Here are some sentence starters you could use in your answer:

- Bishop Odo wanted Robert to be king but most Normans in England did not support him. This made the rebellion easier to defeat because…
- The Church in England supported William Rufus against Odo. For example, Bishop Wulfstan…
- The English people living around Pevensey also supported William. This is shown by…

▶ Pevensey Castle today, where Odo and Robert of Mortain took refuge from William II. Its strong stone defences were added in the 12th century.

Summary

Odo's rebellion of 1088

- Robert Curthose thought he should be king of England as William's eldest son.
- Odo led a rebellion supporting Robert – he thought he could control Robert.
- Most Normans and the English people fought for William II against Odo. Odo and his half brother were defeated.

- Odo held out there too, hoping Robert Curthose would come to support him.
- Help never arrived and he was eventually forced to surrender, as the castle ran out of food and disease spread among the castle defenders.
- Odo was stripped of all his English lands and titles, and exiled.

William was wildly popular after the defeat of Odo and made many promises to his English subjects: lower taxation, an end to the 'forest' and a return to the laws of Edward the Confessor. This list is clearly what the English population had resented most about Norman rule. Unfortunately for the English, William went back on all of them.

3.4 William I and his sons: summary

- William I's strong character definitely influenced the success of the Norman Conquest.
- However, William's strong personality created dangerous tensions between him and his eldest son, Robert.
- It is significant that most Norman barons supported William Rufus against Robert.
- It is significant that the Anglo-Saxon population fought for William II.

Checkpoint

Strengthen

S1 Suggest how William Rufus was able to get Odo to surrender, even though he was in a strong castle.

S2 Explain one reason why William did not think that Robert would be a good duke of Normandy.

Challenge

C1 Explain why you think the majority of Norman barons in England did not support Odo in his rebellion against William Rufus.

How confident do you feel about your answers to these questions? If you are not sure that you answered them well, try the following activity.

Activity

Remembering different individuals and their characteristics can be difficult. Create 'Top History' cards for Anglo-Saxon and Norman England, 1060–88. You will have to decide their scores for a set of key characteristics, for example: Military power, Political influence, Religious power; Economic strength. Key characters would include:

Edward the Confessor, Harold Godwinson, Tostig Godwinson, Edgar Aethling, Harald Hardrada, William the Conqueror, a Norman knight, an English housecarl, a Norman footsoldier, an English fyrdsman, a Norman castellan, Archbishop Stigand, Earls Morcar and Edwin, Earl Waltheof, Hereward the Wake, Bishop Odo, William FitzOsbern, Roger de Breteuil, Ralf de Gael, Malcolm of Scotland, King Sweyn of Denmark, Archbishop Lanfranc, Bishop Wulfstan of Worcester, William Rufus, Robert Curthose and Matilda of Flanders.

Recall quiz

1 'Land held by a vassal in return for service to a lord'. Which key term is that the definition for?

2 How many days a year was knight service for?

3 What was a relief?

4 Stigand was accused of pluralism and simony – which one of these was about appointing people to top Church jobs in exchange for money?

5 What was the demesne?

6 Describe two features of the role of a Norman sheriff.

7 In what year did William order the Domesday Book to be produced?

8 What language replaced English for written documents in Norman England?

9 Outline three key characteristics of William I's personality that help explain the success of the Norman Conquest.

10 What relation was Robert Curthose to Odo?

Exam-style question, Section B

'Of all the changes the Normans made in England, the most important was the change to the Church'.

How far do you agree? Explain your answer.

You may use the following in your answer:

• Lanfranc

• the feudal system.

You **must** also use information of your own. **16 marks**

Exam tip

This question is about importance. When you think about how important a change was, consider the difference that it made: its impact. The most important changes lead to the biggest amount of change. There are some ideas you could use in your answer in the diagram on this page.

Activity

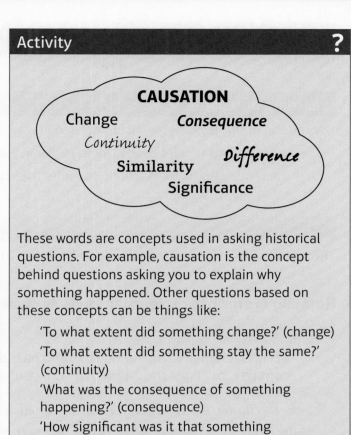

These words are concepts used in asking historical questions. For example, causation is the concept behind questions asking you to explain why something happened. Other questions based on these concepts can be things like:

'To what extent did something change?' (change)

'To what extent did something stay the same?' (continuity)

'What was the consequence of something happening?' (consequence)

'How significant was it that something happened?' (significance)

'How similar was something to something else?' (similarity)

'How different was something to something else?' (difference)

Use each of the words in the word cloud to make a question about Norman England, 1066–88.

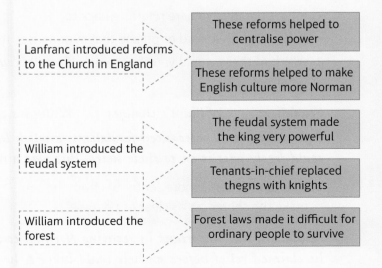

▶ Changes in Norman England.

Writing historically: writing cohesively

When you explain events and their consequences, you need to make your explanation as clear and concise as possible.

Learning outcomes

By the end of this lesson, you will understand how to:

- use pronouns to refer back to ideas earlier in your writing
- use sentence structures to help you refer back to ideas earlier in your writing clearly and economically.

Definitions

Pronoun: a word that can stand in for, and refer back to, a noun, e.g. 'he', 'she', 'this', 'that', etc

How can I refer back to earlier ideas as clearly as possible?

Look at the beginning response to this exam-style question below:

> It was changes in landholding that did the most to secure Norman control of England. How far do you agree? **(16 marks)**

> Before William I introduced feudalism, English land belonged to individual landowners, who could freely pass it on to their heirs. This was a major factor in securing Norman control.

1. In the second sentence, the **pronoun** 'this' refers back to the first sentence. What could it refer back to?

   a. feudalism

   b. ownership of land

   c. passing land to heirs

   d. it's not clear – it could be referring to any or all of them.

One way in which you can improve the clarity of your writing is to avoid imprecise pronouns like 'this' and either:

- repeat the idea you are referring back to OR
- replace it with a word or phrase that summarises the idea.

2. Which of these would you choose to replace 'this' with to make these sentences as clear and precise as possible?

> Feudalism   William's changes   William's changes to landholding   William's idea
>
> Before William I introduced feudalism, English land belonged to individual landowners, who could freely pass it on to their heirs. This was a major factor in securing Norman control.

3. Now look at some more sentences from the same response below. What could you replace 'This' with to make the sentences as clear as possible?

> Feudalism was important in securing Norman control because the king owned all the land, he claimed relief before an heir could inherit, he could claim homage and knight and labour service, and force forfeitures. This enabled him to control his tenants directly.

How can I structure my sentences to make referring back even clearer?

4. Look at three versions below of sentences written in response to the exam-style question on the previous page:

Version A

> *Before the introduction of feudalism, tenants could pass on their land freely to their heirs because they claimed a direct right to the land. This was a significant increase in control because people now only held the land on behalf of the king, who could take it away as easily.*

The pronoun 'this' is meant to refer back to this phrase – but, because it follows this clause, the writer seems to be suggesting that people claiming a direct right to their land significantly increased the king's control!

Version B

> *Tenants could pass on their land freely to their heirs because they claimed a direct right to the land before the introduction of feudalism. This was a significant increase in control because people now only held the land on behalf of the king, who could take it away as easily.*

Version C

> *Tenants could pass on their land freely to their heirs because they claimed a direct right to the land before the introduction of feudalism. This change in landholding was a significant increase in control because people now only held the land on behalf of the king, who could take it away as easily.*

Which version is most clearly expressed and therefore easiest to read? Write a sentence or two explaining your ideas, thinking about:

- the use of the pronoun 'this'
- the position of the idea it refers back to
- the use of a word or phrase that summarises the idea.

Did you notice?

When you read a text, you usually assume that the pronoun 'this' refers back to the piece of information that you have just read – not the one before that, or the one, two or three sentences ago.

5. Why are these sentences below unclear and difficult to make sense of?

> *After Hastings William introduced feudalism. In Anglo-Saxon England earls and other landholders could resist the king as they held their land directly. This greatly increased Norman control.*

Improving an answer

6. Experiment with two or three different ways of rearranging and / or rewriting these sentence fragments to create sentences that explain as clearly as possible why Bishop Odo rebelled against William Rufus.

> *[1] There was a disputed succession [2] when William I died [3] because he divided his lands between his sons and the eldest (Curthose) wanted it all. [4] This resulted in Bishop Odo's rebellion.*

Preparing for your GCSE Paper 2 exam

Paper 2 overview

Paper 2 has two sections. Section B will have your questions on Anglo-Saxon and Norman England. These are worth 20% of your GCSE History assessment. The whole exam is 1 hour 45 minutes. You should use no more than 50 minutes to do section A. That will leave time for Section B, which is your British Depth Study on Anglo-Saxon and Norman England.

History Paper 2	Period Study and British Depth Study			Time 1 hour 45 mins
Section A	Period Study	Answer 3 questions	32 marks	50 mins
Section B	Medieval Depth Options B1 or B2	Answer 3 questions	32 marks	55 mins

Medieval Depth Option B1 Anglo-Saxon and Norman England c1060–88

You will answer Question 4, which is in three parts:

(a) Describe two features of... (4 marks)

You are given a few lines to write about each feature. Allow five minutes to write your answer. It is worth four marks, which means you can keep your answer brief. Do not try to add more information on extra lines.

(b) Explain why... (12 marks)

This question asks you to explain the reasons why something happened. Allow 20 minutes to write your answer. You are given two stimulus (information) points as prompts to help you. You do not have to use the prompts but they might be helpful to give you ideas. Higher marks are gained by explaining a point of your own in addition to the prompts. You will be given at least two pages in the answer booklet for your answer. This does not mean you should try to fill all the space. The front page of the exam paper tells you 'there may be more space than you need'. Aim to give at least three explained reasons.

(c)(i) OR (ii) How far do you agree? (16 marks)

This question is worth half your marks for the whole of the Depth Study. Make sure you have kept 30 minutes to answer it. You have a choice of statements: (i) or (ii). Before you decide, be clear what the statement is about: what 'concept' it is about and what topic information you will need to respond to it. You will have prompts to help as for part (b).

The statement can be about: cause, significance, consequence, change, continuity, similarity or difference. Look at examples of questions to practise working out which of these things the statement is about. You could do this with everyday examples and test one another:

- *the bus was late because it broke down = statement about cause;*
- *the bus broke down as a result of poor maintenance = statement about consequence;*
- *the bus service has improved recently = statement about change.*

You must make a judgement on **how far you agree**. Plan your answer before you begin to write, thinking about points for and against (see the diagram below). You should give at least three points. You must make sure your points all help answer the question.

Don't forget that you must write a conclusion, explaining how much you agree with the statement in the question. For example, you should say what you think was the most important cause, change or consequence and why.

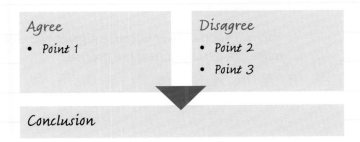

Paper 2, Question 4a

Describe **two** features of towns in Anglo-Saxon England.
(4 marks)

Exam tip

Keep your answer brief. Two points with some extra information about each of them.

Basic answer

Each shire had its main town called a burh which had strong walls. Towns were important for trade.

Identifies two features, but with no supporting information.

4th

Verdict

This is a basic answer because two correct features are given, but there is no supporting information. Use the feedback to rewrite this answer, making as many improvements as you can.

Good answer

The main Anglo-Saxons towns, called burhs, were fortified with strong walls. These protected inhabitants from attack by Viking raiders.

Identifies a correct feature and provides supporting information (protection from attack) that is directly related to it.

7th

Towns were important for trade, especially the burhs. In Anglo-Saxon England, all trade worth a certain amount of money had to take place in burhs by law, so that this trade could be taxed.

Again, the correct feature (that towns were important for trade) is supported with information that relates directly to why this was important.

Verdict

This is a good answer because it gives two clear features of Anglo-Saxon towns and gives extra detail to make the descriptions more precise.

Paper 2, Question 4b

Explain why William won the Battle of Hastings.
You may use the following in your answer:

- knights
- tactics.

You **must** also use information of your own. **(12 marks)**

Exam tip

Focus on explaining 'why'. Aim to give at least three clear reasons.

Basic answer

William won the Battle of Hastings because his army included knights. Knights were warriors who fought on horseback. It took years of training to become a knight because special skills were needed to make a horse run at enemy troops and for the knight to use his lance as his horse charged.

> This is an accurate description, but describing training and skills does not help explain why William won the battle.

Another reason was the Norman tactic of feigned retreat. This was when the Norman troops pretended to run away. When some of Harold's troops saw the Normans running away, they ran after them. The Anglo-Saxons were fooled by the tactic.

> This says the tactic of feigned retreat was a reason why William won the Battle of Hastings, but it does not give an explanation. It needs to say what happened because of the feigned retreat to help William win.

Another reason was William's leadership. When the battle was going against the Normans and it looked like they would be defeated, a rumour spread that William had been killed. He pushed back his helmet to show he was alive and shouted that they would all be killed if they ran away. This made his troops feel more confident and they fought back strongly.

> This is a relevant point and one not suggested in the stimulus bullets. This enables the answer to access higher marks. Providing an example gives support to the point being made. However, while the last line includes a bit of explanation, it is not enough to help the reader clearly understand how William's leadership helped him to win the battle.

William was very lucky to have won the Battle of Hastings in the end because it could easily have been him who was defeated.

> It is valid to say that luck was a factor in William defeating Harold, but the answer doesn't explain why William could easily have been defeated.

Verdict

This is a basic answer because:

- information is accurate, but it is weak because a lot of it is not relevant to the question
- it gives three reasons why William won the Battle of Hastings, but no developed explanations
- some of the answer is focused on the question, but it needs more details and examples.

Use the feedback to rewrite this answer, making as many improvements as you can.

Paper 2, Question 4b

Explain why William won the Battle of Hastings. **(12 marks)**

Good answer

One reason why William won the Battle of Hastings was because his army included knights. The Anglo-Saxon army did not have warriors on horseback, instead they fought on foot using a shield wall. By the end of the battle, knights proved very good at charging through the wall and killing the Anglo-Saxon warriors. This helped William win the Battle of Hastings. After that battle, medieval armies all used knights and no one used shield walls, which proves it was an important reason.

This paragraph gives a clear explanation of why knights helped William win the Battle of Hastings. There is some detail showing knowledge, but more could have been added to support the point about William's knights.

William's tactics were also an important reason for his victory. One tactic was the feigned retreat, which William had used before in battles against the French. This was when Norman troops pretended to run away, so that some of the Anglo-Saxons ran after them. Then the Normans turned round and killed the Anglo-Saxons. It was an important tactic because getting troops to leave the shield wall really weakened the shield wall. Once the shield wall was weakened, William's knights could charge the wall and break it up.

This starts off with a valid point, provides specific information in support and ends with an explanation of how it helped William win, linking it directly to the question.

Another reason was William's leadership. He had planned the invasion very carefully (for example bringing pre-fabricated castles with him), he avoided being trapped in his camp or surprised by Harold's march from London, and he kept trying different tactics (e.g. the feigned retreat) until he found the combination that worked. William was such a good military leader that even Vikings feared to face him in battle.

This adds a new point and supports it effectively, although there could have been a bit more emphasis here on 'explaining why'.

Verdict

This is a good answer because:

- it mainly focuses on the question
- there is no irrelevant background description or unnecessary information
- it supports the reasons with evidence to develop explanations.

The answer could be improved further by clearly linking each point back to why William won the Battle of Hastings.

Paper 2, Question 4c

It was changes in landholding that did the most to secure Norman control of England.

How far do you agree? Explain your answer.

You may use the following in your answer:

- tenants-in-chief
- forfeiture.

You must also use information of your own. **(16 marks)**

Exam tip

Consider points 'For' and 'Against' the statement and make a judgement. Be clear about your reasons for agreeing or disagreeing.

Basic answer

When William became king he said that all the land belonged to him. He kept a lot of the land for himself, including land to go hunting on. Then he gave a lot of land out to tenants-in-chief. They were sometimes called barons. They kept the land in return for paying money to William and fighting for him.

Tenants-in-chief owned over half of the land in England. There were only 190 tenants-in-chief and only two of these were Anglo-Saxons.

Another change to landholding was to do with knights. Lords had to provide knights for William in return for him letting them use 'his' land. That way, William had lots of knights to use in controlling the English population.

So, overall, the statement is correct because the changes in landholding were so important in securing Norman control.

This introduction is unnecessary background information. Nothing in this paragraph answers the question.

The second paragraph gives more details about tenants-in-chief and shows good knowledge. But there isn't any explanation of how tenants-in-chief secured Norman control. The point is made that only two Anglo-Saxons were tenants-in-chief – this could have been used to develop an argument.

This is a good point that comes from the student's own knowledge. It does help answer the question.

The conclusion needs to explain how far landholding was in securing Norman control of England, rather than just stating that the statement is correct.

Verdict

This is a basic answer because:

- it shows some knowledge and understanding of the issue
- not all of the information used is linked to answering the question
- it gives a reason for how Normans secured control, although this is not developed into an explanation
- there is a conclusion, but it is too short and does not say **how far** it was caused by changes in landholding.

Use the feedback to rewrite this answer, making as many improvements as you can.

Paper 2, Question 4c

It was changes in landholding that did the most to secure Norman control of England.
How far do you agree? Explain your answer. **(16 marks)**

Good answer

Landholding did do the most to secure Norman control of England. William rewarded his loyal followers with land: the tenants-in-chiefs. This helped Norman control because William took land from Anglo-Saxons and gave it to Normans. Of the 190 tenants-in-chief in England, only two were Anglo-Saxon. Land was power in Anglo-Saxon and Norman England, so Norman tenants-in-chief meant Normans in power.

William could also use his landholding powers to punish people who did not obey Norman rules or who upset the king. Anyone who rebelled against the king (even those who had fought against William at the Battle of Hastings) forfeited their land. The same was true for the under-tenants of the tenants-in-chief: if they acted against their tenants-in-chief, they could lose their land too. Anglo-Saxons earls who rebelled against William lost their land. This meant other Anglo-Saxons would not want to rebel against Norman control.

However, landholding was not the only way in which Norman control of England was secured. Castles were also important. For example, castles gave the Normans secure bases to dominate areas of England. Without castles, it is not likely that Normans would have kept control over England.

I believe that changes in landholding were the most important. Land was the key to wealth and power and William made sure that only those loyal to the Norman regime had it.

The introduction shows that the student is focused on the question, including the 'how far' part of the question.

The student moves onto another reason in paragraph 2. This is a valid reason that is developed with good detail. Again, the student stays focused on answering the question.

This paragraph introduces another reason from the student's own knowledge. This is important for getting the best marks. The point is valid but it could use some more detail to develop it into an explanation.

The student states 'how far' they agree with the statement and sums up the reason why they think this.

Verdict

This is a good answer because:

- it answers the question directly
- it gives a reason other than those mentioned in the question
- two explanations have been developed and supported with accurate and precise evidence
- the conclusion answers how far landholding did the most.

The answer could be improved further by developing the third point and expanding the conclusion so it explains why landholding was more important than castles.

Answers to Recall Quiz questions

Chapter 1

1   Edward the Confessor.

2   Norway.

3   Tostig, Gyrth, Leofwine [Wulfnoth and Sweyn also valid, but not mentioned in the chapter. Sweyn was Harold's eldest brother (Earl of Hereford), d.1052].

4   An Anglo-Saxon fortified town.

5   A thegn.

6   Harold Godwinson, William of Normandy, Harald Hardrada and Edgar Aethling.

7   Harald Hardrada (and Tostig).

8   King Harold II (Harold Godwinson).

9   One from the following: feigned retreat; cavalry (knights) charges against the shield wall; using archers, foot soldiers and cavalry flexibly; moving archers to closer range once the Anglo-Saxon shield wall had been broken up.

10 Gyrth, Earl of East Anglia and Leofwine, Earl of the south-west Midlands (who was also Earl of Kent later).

Chapter 2

1   Edgar Aethling.

2   Berkhamstead (and possibly also Barking for Earls Edwin and Morcar).

3   Hereford, Shrewsbury, Chester.

4   Answers could include: the keep; the motte (earthen mound); wooden palisades; access to the keep (steps or bridge); the ditch; the gatehouse (or drawbridge).

5   Edgar (Maerleswein and Gospatric also escaped with him).

6   Burning crops in the fields, destroying seed crops and killing livestock to make life impossible in the region.

7   The three ways given in the text are: by forfeit, through the creation of new earldoms and other blocks of territory, and through illegal land grabs. Lands also got transferred through inheritance (Normans being made heirs to Anglo-Saxon lands) and through marriage (when Anglo-Saxon wives brought land to Norman husbands).

8   Ralph de Gael (Earl of East Anglia), Roger de Breteuil (Earl of Hereford) and Waltheof (Earl of Northumbria).

9   Ralph de Gael escaped to Brittany, Roger de Breteuil was put in prison for life by William, and Waltheof fled abroad. Waltheof was lured back, imprisoned, and then executed in 1076.

10 Archbishop Lanfranc – as William's regent.

Chapter 3

1   A fief (or a feud).

2   40 days.

3   A payment that a Norman heir had to make to the king when they inherited land.

4   Simony.

5   The land that the king or a tenant kept for his own use rather than granting it as a fief to an under-tenant.

6   Answers could include: the representative of the king; the leader of the shire; oversaw the shire court; enforced the law; responsible for organising the fyrd; responsible for the military defences of the shire.

7   1085 (Christmas), the first drafts were ready in 1086.

8   Latin.

9   Answers could include: he was relentless – he never gave up; he was brutal – he used excessive force, which helped crush resistance; he demanded loyalty – he imprisoned Odo once he appeared to challenge William; he had always had to fight for survival – which made him paranoid about any threat to his rule; he was religious – which helped gain the pope's support; he loved money – which drove him on to make the Conquest a success.

10 Odo was Robert Curthose's uncle. Odo was Williams I's half-brother. Robert Curthose was William I's son.

Acknowledgements

Picture Credits:

(Key: b-bottom; c-centre; l-left; r-right; t-top)

Alamy: Glenn Harper 95, Justin Kase z12z 55, Pictorial Press Ltd 6, 11, QEDimages 90, Skyscan Photolibrary 7t, Walter Rawlings/Robertharding Cover, 35, World History Archive 25, Timewatch Images 16, The Art Archive 3, 58; **Getty Images**: Andrea Ricordi/Moment 97, DeAgostini/Dea Pictures Library 30, Heritage Images/Hulton Fine Art Collection 63, Pawel Toczynski/ The Image Bank Unreleased 91, PHAS/Universal Images Group 78, Print Collector/Hulton Archive 17, Susandaniels/iStock 42; **Mary Evans Picture Library**: Mary Evans/The National Archives, London. England. 74, 88; **The Bridgeman Art Library Ltd**: © British Library Board. All Rights Reserved 8, 13.

All other images © Pearson Education

Text

J. M. Dent and Sons Ltd: G.N. Garmonsway, The Anglo-Saxon Chronicle, © 1975, J. M. Dent and Sons Ltd. Used with Permission. 45, 51, 68, 88, 94; **Oxford University Press**: Kevin Crossley-Holland, The Anglo-Saxon World: An Anthology, ISBN 9780192835475, © 1999, Oxford University Press 4, 39.